A Difficult Grace

The Life of Poetry

POETS ON THEIR ART AND CRAFT

A Difficult Grace

ON POETS, POETRY, AND WRITING

Michael Ryan

THE UNIVERSITY OF GEORGIA PRESS

ATHENS AND LONDON

Published by the University of Georgia Press

Athens, Georgia 30602

© 2000 by Michael Ryan

Designed by Betty Palmer McDaniel

Set in 10/13 Minion by G&S Typesetters, Inc.

Printed and bound by McNaughton and Gunn

The paper in this book meets the guidelines for
permanence and durability of the Committee on
Production Guidelines for Book Longevity of the
Council on Library Resources.

Printed in the United States of America

04   03   02   01   00   C   5   4   3   2   1

04   03   02   01   00   P   5   4   3   2   1

Library of Congress Cataloging-in-Publication Data

Ryan, Michael, 1946–

   A difficult grace : on poets, poetry, and writing /
Michael Ryan.

     p. cm.

   Includes bibliographical references and index.

   ISBN 0-8203-2264-4 (alk. paper)

   ISBN 0-8203-2231-8 (pbk. : alk. paper)

   1. Poetry.   I. Title.

   PS324 .A6 2000

811.009 — dc21   00-026110

British Library Cataloging-in-Publication Data available

CONTENTS

PREFACE

Abook of essays by a contemporary poet might be expected to be about contemporary poetry, and this one certainly is, but with the exceptions of essays on Donald Justice and Stanley Kunitz and a few illustrative references, the names of living poets do not appear here. I wrote most of these essays to understand the poets who have formed most of my own poetic assumptions: essentially, but not exclusively (and abundantly commingled), Dickinson, Yeats, Pound, Eliot, Williams, Whitman, Frost, Bishop, and Stevens. Although these poets have already generated libraries of criticism, to which I'm indebted, I hoped to discover and articulate for myself how these particular people wrote their particular poems. I wanted, as much as I could, to absorb them. This desire provoked serial immersions in their work, then led me to search for where they got *their* assumptions, which generated the study that resulted in the first and longest essay in this book. I learned that in the best writers technique is an embodied expression of belief, and that style rooted in necessity can be the fullest communication not just of the writer's ideas but of his or her whole being. Consequently, the idea of "progress" in art, that there ever has been or could be an "avant-garde," came to seem to me little more than a sentimentalization of the role of the artist in our culture, and a misapplication of an uncritical faith in "advances" in science, technology, and expansionist capitalist economics that has infected very much thinking and writing, including about poetry, showing itself most obviously in the current valuation of self-displaying "originality" over authenticity. Whereas there's no question that a poet, like any other human being, is permeated by his or her historical moment, ethnicity, gender, class, and childhood experience, what I am most drawn to in what I read makes all that seem incidental. The writer's material is essential, but what really matters to me is what he or she makes of it. The writing I love most is finally about the reader not the writer.

Writing an autobiography was for me the greatest challenge to this conviction, the truth of which I believed ought to apply to personal narrative no less than to lyric poetry, and the experience of writing my autobiography generated the second- and third-to-last essays in this book. The final essay—"Vocation According to Dickinson"—takes up the main subject touched throughout the book and uses Emily Dickinson as a guide through the sometimes bewildering conflation of vocation and career. I left out of this essay a comparison of the etymologies of the two words. "Vocation," as most readers of this book know, means "a divine calling to a religious life." A "career" is a racecourse.

A Difficult Grace

POETRY AND THE AUDIENCE

There's a moment I love in *The Public Enemy,* starring James Cagney. Rocky has come home a hero from the Great War and moved back into the family's coldwater flat with his poor, widowed, good-hearted Irish mother. Cocky and ambitious but unable to get better than menial jobs, increasingly humiliated, frustrated, and angry, he falls in with what his poor, widowed, good-hearted Irish mother never tires of calling "the wrong crowd," rolling both *r*s heartily in her stage-Irish brogue. She nags him constantly about it, against all odds and the demands of the plot and the producer, until Rocky's patience (which has far exceeded ours) gives out, and he turns to her and snaps, "What do you want me to do, stay at home all day and write *poems?*" At the end of the movie, after we've witnessed his rise and fall in a life of crime, he is machine-gunned on the steps of the cathedral and dies in the arms of his mistreated-but-ever-faithful girlfriend. A passerby asks, "Who is this guy anyway?" And she looks up mournfully and answers, "He used to be a big shot." Camera pans back. Music up. Fade out. The End.

When the houselights go on, I have wanted to stand up and ask the audience, "Now wouldn't Rocky have been better off staying at home and writing poems?" But I'm like the Bushman to whom the anthropologists showed the film of the jumbo jet: he was more excited by the few frames in which a barely visible rabbit happened to scurry across the runway. The rabbit was his tribe's sacred animal. The anthropologists hadn't noticed it in the film. And even if the audience

1

did recall Rocky's opinion of poets by the time the movie was over, someone could answer, "No, he wouldn't have been better off. Instead of being machine-gunned he would have starved. Or he would have kept his rotten jobs, suffered poverty and humiliation, and how would he have found time to write anyway? Besides, he would have never been a big shot."

But anthropology has shown us many cultures in which poets were "big shots." In aboriginal tribes, extant and extinct, the poet is usually the central figure, the shaman-healer. Because he is close to the gods, through his "divine madness," he keeps the tribe together by celebrating in his chants and sacred rituals its shared beliefs, ancestry, and cosmology. The tribe depends on the poet for its life.

The roots of poetry, as well as of dance and drama, are in performances of myth and magic that have a religious purpose and socially cohesive effect. As Jane Ellen Harrison says in *Ancient Art and Ritual,*

> Art is social in origins. The dance from which the drama rose was
> a choral dance . . . what the Greeks called a *thiaros.* The word
> means a bond and a thing of devotion; and reverence, devotion,
> collective emotion, is social in its very being.

According to Harrison, it's not at all what the individual feels but "what the tribe feels that is sacred." This may be difficult for Rocky (and us) to understand, stuck as we are in the middle of a powerful industrial capitalist culture in which the primacy of self and the ostensibly inalienable rights of the individual are two essential elements of the encompassing myth. The language of myth, through the metaphors of poetry and drama or science and sports, communicates the values the culture says we must adopt to survive. In a society in which cooperation is required to kill the meat and gather the vegetables, the myths subordinate the individual to the tribe. The individual can't survive outside the tribe and the tribe can't survive individualism. For the Maori, according to anthropologists, it would in fact be more accurate to say that there is no such thing as an "individual."

In such preliterate societies, even those as late as ancient Greece and Anglo-Saxon England, the poet is the ideologue, historian, theologian, philosopher, TV, newspaper, Internet, and megamultiplex cinema rolled into one. Maybe putting it in these terms dramatizes what the poet is *not* in contemporary American culture and the size of the audience he would have if he were. But industrial capitalism is only one of the more recent forces that have swept across what was originally the poet's territory and pushed him into the lyric corner where he's ignored by the culture at large. The tribe was interested in what the poet had to say because his subject was the tribe. There are still remnants of this in Chaucer, but *The Canterbury Tales* is the first modern poem in England not only because of its interest in the individual in society but also because it was written to be read. In preliterate societies, in which poetry was orally transmitted, a strict mnemonic regularity (whether of Anglo-Saxon alliterative accentuals or Homeric dactylic hexameters) was an essential feature of the verse, for the sake of *its* survival in the memory of the listeners no less than its dramatic effect. Authorship was probably neither entirely individual nor collective. *The Iliad* and *The Odyssey* were probably composed over hundreds of years, the work of many bards. Not coincidentally, both poems take every opportunity to praise such bards, and, since they wandered from place to place reciting their tales, hospitality to strangers is put forth in the poems as a major virtue. Odysseus says in book IX of *The Odyssey*,

> I think life is at its best when a whole people is in festivity and banqueters in the hall sit next to each other listening to the bard, while the tables by them are laden with wine and meat, and the cupbearer draws wine from the mixing bowl and pours it into the cups. That, I think, is the happiest thing there is.

A commercial message, built into the story, delivered by the hero. From our vantage, the fact of its presence indicates that in this incipient period of Greek civilization—when the vases were painted solely with geometric designs and the sculpture was still rigid, left foot in front of right foot and arms stiff at the sides in the archaic mode—the poet was already well on his way in his fall from grace.

In the first century A.D. in Ireland, there was a class of learned men, the *file*, who also made it their task in life to preserve ancient stories. The most distinguished kind of *file*, the *ollamh*, was master of two hundred fifty major narratives and one hundred minor ones. Yeats refers to this tradition in "Under Ben Bulben," one of his last poems, when he exhorts, "Irish poets, learn your trade." By the time of the *file*, at least in Europe, poetry was a profession. Although his position was no longer central, the poet still had an essential and therefore prestigious social role. According to the historian Daniel Boorstin:

> Before the printed book, Memory ruled daily life and the occult learning, and fully deserved the name later applied to printing, the "art preservative of all the arts." The Memory of individuals and of communities carried knowledge through time and space. . . .
> By Memory and in Memory the fruits of education were garnered, preserved, and stored.

The *file* were the libraries and the entertainment, the repositories of information and wisdom, and they were largely responsible for what social cohesion there was. Consequently, the identity of the individual poet was nothing in light of the social function of his poetry. A particular narrative survived only if it served that social function, which in turn depended on how engaging and memorable the story was made. The poem was tested on the audience and modified from its response. The same stories were told over and over again, the stories that concerned everyone. They had to contain *literally* enduring qualities, of both narrative and style. As Gilbert Murray says in *The Classical Tradition in Poetry*, "The manner of the Heroic Age is that of poets who know what they are describing and audiences that know the thing that is being talked about," and this manner is characterized by "temperance and sobriety of invention." The style's subordination to the subject, the author's self-effacement for the sake of the story, is intimately connected to his social role, a role that's as secure as his clear rendering of the thing.

It's not as if the possibility of flashy language and self-display never occurred to these poets. In Book II of *The Iliad*, we hear of Thamyris the Thracian who boasted of a newfangled sort of poetry to surpass the Muses: "And they in wrath made him a maimed man, and took away from him his heavenly song and made him forget his harping." If Homer's line is read with the sense of timeless mythic time (*in illo tempore*), it tells us that the egoism of Thamyris means his heavenly song is already lost.

Given that the social role of the poet now bears about as much resemblance to his role in the Heroic Age as contemporary America does to ancient Greece, it's remarkable that those enduring qualities we think of as "classical"—the subordination of style to subject, "temperance and sobriety of invention"—have in fact endured into our century. In Pound's dicta they appear as "objectivity—and, again—objectivity," "direct treatment of the thing," and his relentless exhortation in his early essays to clarity and precision. Eliot's self-classified "classicism in literature" is certainly behind his "objective correlative" as working method, his sense of the importance and value of tradition, and his principal beliefs that "the emotion of art is impersonal" and "permanent literature is always a presentation."

For both Pound and Eliot, these are not merely aesthetic impulses without social implications. But their "classicism" was nothing Homer would have recognized. *The Waste Land* is hardly characterized by "temperance and sobriety of invention." Yeats recorded his initial response to the poem in a 1924 preface dedicated to Lady Gregory: "The other day when I read that strange 'Waste Land' by Mr. T. C. [!] Eliot I thought of your work and Synge's; and he is American born and Englishman bred, and writes but of his own mind." The dislocation Yeats perceived in Eliot's poem he attributed to a dislocation of place, a disconnection from "the soil" that so concerned the Irish Literary Revival. For Yeats, poetry couldn't exist without an actual, defined audience to ground it. Just who that audience was vacillated in Yeats's mind between the peasantry and the aristocracy, from writing "as an Irish writer and with Ireland in my mind" to writing for an elite international "audience, 'fit though few,' which is greater than any nation, for it is made up of chosen persons from all." At other times, he declared that his ideal audience was, respectively, "the town of Sligo," "young men between twenty and thirty," "a few friends [for whom] one always writes," and "a man who does not exist, / a man who is but a dream." No doubt Yeats was (as he said himself) as "anarchic as a sparrow," and his invention of his much-discussed "masks" may have come from his difficulty adopting an "essential stance" toward an audience for longer than the moment of a single poem. But Yeats initially faced in Ireland the same problem regarding an audience for his poetry that Eliot and Pound faced in England and Williams and Stevens faced in the United States: there was none. Pound believed a good book of poems could never sell more than five hundred copies; Stevens's first book, *Harmonium,* in fact sold less than one hundred copies; and Williams's early books sold so badly that he entitled one *Al Que Quiere* ("to him who wants it"). These poets responded in various ways to this common situation, and each poet's response bears a direct relationship to the poetry he wrote: its style, subjects, structure, tone, even its syntax—in short, its whole character. The poet's idea of his audience (which may or may not be accurate) is fused to his idea of his cultural role (which may or may not be realistic) and thereby influences and sometimes even generates his poetry.

Of all American poets, this is most visible in Whitman, since he most explicitly embraces his audience and his cultural role as part of the subject of his poem. By his own testimony,

> "Leaves of Grass," before a line was written, presupposed something different from any other, and, as it stands, is the result of such presupposition.

Crucial to this "presupposition" was the audience he hoped the poem would reach and the cultural and political role he hoped the poem would play. In this regard, it's the conservative Frost, not the liberal Williams, who is Whitman's heir, although Frost is certainly a bastard son, his own preferred genealogy being Palgrave's *Treasury* and Long-fellow, not Whitman and his suspicious ideas of democracy, sexuality, and poetic form. As Frost said, he wanted to "get the poems over" to "the general reader who buys books in the thousands." He wrote from England in 1913 that he had no wish to be "caviar to the crowd the way my quasi-friend Pound does."

But if Frost's idea of his audience approached Whitman's, the poetry it generated to carry out his program could not have been more different. "Poetry is the one permissible way of saying one thing and meaning another": Frost's notion of metaphor, at the heart of his poetics, makes the poet less a prophet than a Trickster. He wrote to Untermeyer in 1917 that "all the fun is outside saying things that suggest formulae that won't formulate—that almost but don't quite formulate." Frost is referring here to the style he plans to use in his new teaching position at Amherst, but his remarks also apply to the poetry he is writing. He goes on to say:

> I should like to be so subtle at this game as to seem to the earnest
> person altogether obvious. The earnest person would assume
> I meant nothing or else came near enough meaning something
> he was familiar with to mean it for all practical purposes. Well,
> well, well.

Edward Thomas, reviewing *North of Boston* in 1914, praised its "freedom from 'audience,' from the sense that there was a reader out there to be entertained or cajoled or even 'bullied,'" and praised Frost for writing with "no purpose beyond expressing" his deepest concerns. Set against the poems in *New Hampshire* that Frost wrote between 1916 and 1923 and that show (in Randall Jarrell's words) "the public figure's relishing consciousness of himself," Thomas's review can be read as a gentle exhortation to a friend about the hazards of his ambition for a general audience for his poetry.

While Frost had a firm, shrewd estimate of the character of that audience and set himself in a relationship to it that was aggressively self-protective, Yeats's vacillations belie the endurance, clarity, and strength of his conviction that the connection between poetry and its audience is inevitable and straightforward. As Frost's audience grew larger and larger, his work became more often ceremonious and self-conscious. As Yeats became "a smiling public man," his poetry cut closer to the bone. As early as his first book of essays, *Ideas of Good and Evil* (1903), while his work was still under the specialized influences of the *fin-de-siècle* cult of Beauty and the mystical Order of the Golden Dawn, Yeats nonetheless wrote: "Does not the greatest poetry always require a people to listen to it?" That is, not only does the poet require an audience, but the *poetry* requires an audience, so that *it* does not become "accidental and temporary," abstract, peripheral, precious, cut off from central human concerns, so that the poet does not "write but of his own mind" (like Mr. T. C. Eliot).

Yeats came to this view through visiting the country people with Lady Gregory to collect stories for her volumes of Irish folklore, and through his efforts with her to establish the Abbey Theater and promote an Irish Literary Revival. He wrote in 1906:

> My work in Ireland has continually set this thought before me: "How can I make my work mean something to vigorous and simple men when attention is not given to art but to a shop, or teaching in a National School, or dispensing Medicine?" I had not wanted to "elevate them" or "educate them," as these words are understood, but to make them understand my vision, and I had not wanted a large audience, certainly not what is called a national audience, but for enough people for what is accidental and temporary to lose itself in the lump. . . . I have always come to this certainty: what moves natural men in the arts is what moves them in life, and that is, intensity of personal life, intonations that show them, in a book or a play, the strength, the essential moment of a man who would be exciting in the market or at the dispensary door.

As he said in "A General Introduction for My Work" over thirty years later, he therefore "tried to make the language of poetry coincide with that of passionate, normal speech" and sought "a powerful, passionate syntax" for "a poetry stripped of rhetoric, like a cry from the heart." (The last quotation is from his speech to the *Poetry* banquet in 1914.)

Pound would seem to have disagreed with none of Yeats's ideas about poetry. From 1913 to 1916, he spent the winters in Sussex as Yeats's secretary, and for the ten years preceding had regarded Yeats as indisputably the greatest living poet. Pound wrote to Harriet Monroe in January 1915 that the language of poetry ought to depart "in no way from speech save by a heightened intensity (ie simplicity)," and there should be "no Tennysonianess of speech; nothing—nothing that you couldn't, in some circumstance, in the stress of some emotion, actually say." Pound's views, coming from Yeats's cottage, are views Yeats had held for some time. Yet no poetry would eventually be more different from Yeats's poetry than Pound's.

In both structure and content, these differences come from their dissimilar notions of the audience. Despite his sentimental attachment to the idea of aristocracy, Yeats believed the vitality of poetry must be drawn from common life—this is why the audience is essential to the poetry, as well as to the poet. For Pound, the opposite is the case:

> The artist is not dependent on the multitude of his listeners. Humanity is the rich effluvium, it is the waste and manure and the soil, and from it grows the tree of the arts. . . .
>
> It is true that the great artist has in the end always, his audience, for the Lord of the universe sends into this world in each generation a few intelligent spirits, and these ultimately manage the rest. But this rest—this rabble, this multitude—does not create the great artist. They are aimless and drifting without him. They dare not inspect their own souls.

This is twenty years but only a goose step away from Mussolini's chamber, where Pound was welcomed as the great poet, although, as the story is told, Mussolini had never read a word of Pound's poetry. He wouldn't have been able to understand it anyway. Pound's essay, entitled "The Audience," appeared in *Poetry* in 1914, written in response to Harriet Monroe's adopting as a motto for the magazine Whitman's line: "To have great poetry there must be great audiences, too." Seeing the motto on the back cover every month irked Pound no end, and he lobbied doggedly for its removal. In his view, poetry is a communication, but "a communication between Intelligent Men." The audience is a tiny elite group who, by means he doesn't articulate, "manage the rest."

This cultural version of right-wing economics becomes the main theme of *The Cantos*. From the beginning, Pound wrote poems not about poetry (as did Stevens) but about the poem's progress and reception in the world. What Yeats feared most about losing contact with "natural men" is surely realized in the structure and subject of

The Cantos, even if they are also sometimes "passionate speech" (or fragments of it), especially those written while Pound was without his books in the detention camp at Pisa. Art and its degradation in a botched civilization is the subject Pound was most passionate about. When Pound arrived in England in 1908, the most popular poets were Noyes, Kipling, Watson, and Newbolt. Their newspaper verses exhorted England to more imperial conquests. In the United States, Longfellow's influence was still considerable, the public was buying James Whitcomb Riley (whom Pound, bizarrely, admired), and in the universities a watery academic romanticism prevailed (this was Williams's and Stevens's earliest model). Pound devoted his fanatic's energy to putting across his idea of the seriousness and cultural value of poetry. In 1919 alone, he published one hundred and nine reviews, articles, and essays.

As early as 1913, chastising Harriet Monroe (as usual), Pound wrote:

> It is increasingly hard to maintain an interest in "the american reader." GORRD! . . . I have no intention of conceding an inch. The public is stupid, and any other opening, from me, would be the rankest hypocrisy.

His pessimism, and his arrogance, could only deepen. Ten years later, soliciting contributions to establish an annuity for Eliot so he could quit his job at the bank, Pound began his "Bel Esprit" circular: "There is no organized or coordinated civilization left, only individual scattered survivors. Aristocracy is gone, its function was to select." In yet another ten years, he would write in a letter: "Don't knock Mussolini, at least not until you have weighed up the obstacles and necessities of the time. He will end up with Sigismundo and the men of order." Sigismundo Malatesta, a quattrocento patron of the arts and egomaniacal tyrant whose use of terror makes Cesare Borgia look like Mother Teresa, became one of the heroes of *The Cantos.*

Pound's moral universe is a curious, ugly place, and his politics are of a piece with his idea of poetry and the audience. The modernist revolution in poetry was a right-wing coup, and many "postmodern" poets who have followed seem to have accepted modernist aesthetic assumptions without considering the political or ethical implications of those assumptions, as if art existed either in a vacuum or in its own high kingdom apart from the rest of human life. The fact that Pound was a Fascist and that most of the poets of his generation—Yeats, Frost, Stevens, Eliot, Lawrence, and Jeffers—had aristocratic, reactionary, "royalist," or explicitly Fascist affiliations between the wars can't be explained away by "the obstacles and necessities of the time." Even if the sorry quality of work by their counterparts on the left (Sandburg and Lindsay, for example, both of whom Monroe championed) argues for a certain distance of the modern poet from mass culture, too much distance clearly results in an insular, genteel poetry in which the linguistic surfaces become glittery, experience privileged, subjects agreeable, and emotions tepid. Of Pound's generation, only Williams was a democrat, and he says in his *Autobiography:* "The great world never very much interested me." Although Williams complained mightily about the public indifference to poetry, his temperament and bang-em-out aesthetics seem to have been luckily suited to his life: "As far as the writing itself is concerned, it takes next to no time at all. . . . There is always time to bang out a few pages." (Between seeing patients in his office he wrote on a typewriter he'd raise to desk-level and lower into the typewriter stand and hide from view by means of a crank. He didn't want them to think they weren't getting his full attention.) Stevens also seems to have been content enough to write his poetry before nine and after five, but only after his first years in New York without secure employment, which he recorded in his journal as "living a strange, insane kind of life." The others found themselves in conflict with a culture in which until well past middle age they had to struggle to live and write and could not support themselves as poets.

Pound seems to have felt this conflict most intensely, and to have been least able to accept it. Here are a few more lines from the "Bel Esprit" circular:

Darkness and confusion as in Middle Ages; no chance of general order or justice; we can only release an individual here and there.

Only thing we can give the artist is leisure to work in. Only way we can get work from him is to assure him this leisure.

. . . Every writer is penalized for not printing EVERYTHING he can sell.

Eliot, in bank, makes 500. Too tired to write, broke down; during convalescence in Switzerland did *Waste Land,* a masterpiece; one of the most important 19 pages in English. Returned to bank, and is again gone to pieces, physically.

Must restart civilization. . . .

Pound believed for his whole life that the world had come to an end, but even to his circle of initiates it must have been astonishing that he thought he could actually "restart civilization" by giving T. S. Eliot time to write poetry. Pound's inflation of the poet's role, his evangelical faith in the word, is the source of intensity, poignancy, and bombast in his work, bombast that in its own way makes the worst of Matthew Arnold seem like dry understatement. It is as if he spent most waking moments and all dreaming ones trying to make the world possible for poetry.

But if Pound and Eliot didn't "restart civilization," they did, for their part, restart poetry. As Williams said bitterly, "*The Waste Land* returned us to the classroom." Williams of course meant his remark figuratively, although in fact the university had since become exile's island, at least in the United States after World War II, when the GI Bill and the country's industrial dominance of the world caused colleges to burgeon overwhelmingly overnight. But poets were never really repatriated after Plato banished them from the State for being liars. For Plato, language must be used in civilized society to communicate rational ideas for orderly purposes, and this, as he well knew (since he wrote some poems himself), is not how it's used in poetry. In poetry, according to Plato, "a god speaks through the mouth of a man," hence poetry is potentially dangerous to a rule of law dependent upon the rational agreement of citizens. In some cultures, this is still thought to be true and poets are silenced. Except to a few NEA-bashing Congressmen, this is unthinkable here, less because of our enlightenment than (in Czeslaw Milosz's words) "the unspoken assumption that the influence of the written word on institutions and morals is nonexistent." Especially if the written word appears in the form of verse. In the countries in which poetry retains the least remnant of its archaic social power there are poets in prison.

The point at which poetry finally lost its social role in England is usually traced to the Industrial Revolution. The aesthetic response of the English Romantics to their lack of audience—articulated in poems and essays by Wordsworth, Coleridge, and Shelley, letters by Keats, and lectures by Hazlitt—continues to dominate our own poetic assumptions two hundred years later. This is because the cultural position of poetry is essentially the same now as it was then, despite the otherwise overwhelming changes since that time in the texture of daily life, the discoveries of science, and the evolution of habits and values and ways we see ourselves and the world. Notwithstanding the efforts of Emerson and Whitman, poetry never played a significant role in forming social values in the United States.

But the audience had begun its exit with the invention of movable type over three hundred years before the Industrial Revolution and the Romantic reaction to it. As Auden says in his trenchant introductions to the five-volume *Viking Poets of the English Language,* "Anglo-Saxon is the poetry of a tribe; Elizabethan poetry is the poetry of a nation." Tribal poetry is oral; as soon as writing is published, poetry is read not heard, and reading is a skill that must be learned in leisure and is therefore a privilege of those who have leisure— namely, the king, the clergy, the aristocracy, and, later on, wealthy merchants and bailiffs of manors. The concept of universal education, even for Caucasian men only, didn't appear until the French Revolution. The province of poetry was the court, the rich and powerful, the aristocracy Yeats and Pound were nostalgic for. Court poetry, composed to be read, very quickly became intellectually ingenious to distinguish itself from the ballads continuing the oral tradition among the common folk. Auden says:

> We are so accustomed to a culture in which poetry is the high-
> brow medium, to be employed for communicating the most in-
> tense and subtle experiences, while the medium for everyday use
> is prose, that it is difficult for us to imagine a society [i.e., before
> 1300] in which the relative positions were the other way round, a

time when verse was the popular medium for instruction and entertainment and prose, mostly Latin, the specialized medium for the intercourse of scholars.

By 1580, literacy was general among the nobility, the positions of prose and poetry had reversed, and the social utility of poetry was already in question. Sidney says in his *Apology:* "I have just cause to make a pitiful defense of poor Poetry, which from almost the highest estimation of learning, is fallen to be the laughingstock of children." His defense, borrowed from Horace (who found himself in a similar situation), is that the social value of poetry derives from its ability to teach and delight: "Delight to move men to take that goodness in hand . . . and teach, to make them know that goodness whereunto they are moved." In other words, the social value of poetry lies in its efficacy as an instrument of knowledge and propaganda (without, for Sir Philip, the pejorative connotations of the latter term). Poetry and poets can be useful to society by identifying its moral ideas ("virtue") and causing citizens to believe in them.

It was a brilliant maneuver, and held as the predominant justification for poetry until Wordsworth and beyond. Although reading made contact with poetry a solitary pleasure instead of a communal entertainment, and poetry was no longer needed to store and preserve knowledge, Sidney's poet theoretically serves one part of the social role of the Irish *file:* to dispense communal wisdom in an entertaining fashion.

Of course, it did not work out that way at all. The voice of the poet immediately became individual and personal, the dominant poetic mode lyric instead of narrative, poetic diction more refined and less like common speech, and poetic logic and structure more elaborate and less spontaneous. Elizabethan poetry was composed by a courtier or clergyman in a room by himself with his own thoughts, most often of his mistress or his God. The ballad tradition persisted among the lower classes, but, without a power base and therefore "moral" function, ballads became mere entertainment, usually bawdy entertainment, and soon evolved into broadsides and newspaper verse. Though Sidney's poet serves a very small audience (the court and nobles), it's a real and powerful one to whom he is at least theoretically important. Ben Jonson put the reigning idea with characteristic economy: "A Prince without Letters is a Pilot without eyes. All his Government is grasping."

In his *Apology,* Sidney performs a piece of sophistry worth noting because it shows how he must revise Plato's idea of poetry to keep poetry theoretically connected to the audience and useful to a civilized society. First, he affirms Plato himself "depended most of poetry" and is himself "of all philosophers . . . the most poetical." Then Sidney argues that poets can't be liars because they do not labor "to tell you what is, or is not, but what should or should not be," adding that Plato meant to banish only the "abuse" of poetry (its causing wrong opinion), not the thing itself. Throughout, Sidney divorces Plato from his interpreters (a polemical strategy whose classical roots Sidney's contemporaries would have recognized), and ends this part of his argument with a key passage:

> So as Plato, banishing the abuse, not the thing, not banishing it, but giving due honor unto it, shall be our patron, and not our adversary. For indeed I had much rather (sith truly I may do it,) show their mistaking of Plato, (under whose lion's skin they would make an asslike braying against poesy,) than go about to overthrow his authority, whom the wiser a man is, the more just cause he shall find to have in admiration; especially, *sith he attributeth unto poesy, more than myself do; namely, to be the very inspiring of a divine force, far above man's wit.* (my italics)

To speak to a civilized audience, and be socially functional, Sidney turns poetry into a civilized activity. Rather than Plato's embodiment of a divine, unruly, dangerous force, it becomes for the sake of a moral and social good the expression of man's "wit" (which Hobbes defined a few years later as the "swift succession of one thought to another and steddy direction to some approved end").

Keeping Hobbes's definition in mind, the line from Sir Philip Sidney to Dr. Samuel Johnson can be seen as a straight one, despite the proliferation of individual styles during the two hundred years that separate them. Auden says:

The real novelty in Romantic poetry is not its diction but its structure. If the Romantic poets, after rejecting Pope and Dryden, did not rediscover Donne and the Metaphysical poets, this was because the latter, no less than the former, organized their poems logically.

A radical change in diction like Wordsworth's in fact forces a radical adjustment in structure, but Wordsworth and Coleridge did see clearly that "wit" was above all a structural principle that had to be overturned for its political no less than its poetic implications. For Sidney, the social value of "wit" ("the steddy direction to some approved end") is the foundation of its poetic value. By means of "wit," the shared moral values (the "approved end" of "virtue") are enacted by the poems. Without this social and moral foundation, poetry is frivolous and potentially harmful. For Samuel Johnson, *every* aesthetic value implies and requires such a base—hence his moral criticism of Shakespeare's "rough numbers," a poet's duty being reflected even in his prosody. To us, this may seem the *reductio ad absurdum* of the elevation of wit, but if poetic values are not based on moral values approved by the society, the poetry has no immediate authority, no social function, and no audience, and this was the overriding, legitimate concern for poets from Sidney to Johnson. When the Romantics replaced "wit" with the "imagination of the Poet," individual and unbounded, as the structural or, as Coleridge called it, the "architectonic" faculty, theoretically they did so at this expense.

In practice, as soon as poetry had been composed in writing and preserved in books, as soon as the wisdom and knowledge of the race did not need to be remembered with the aid and through the forms of stories-in-verse, poetry could and did become less and less important to the business of society. This situation, first lamented in England by Sidney, appears to us to have resulted in a great period of poetry. In the Elizabethan lyric alone, new prosodies were invented for songs and meditations, and many stanza forms developed from the sonnet in response to developments in music and logic (even though the greatest richness was the blank verse written for a thriving stage). If wit in Shakespeare's time was sometimes confused with ingenuity, by the eighteenth century its essential structural role in composition was firmly established, probably peaking in Pope's "Essay On Criticism," in which the word itself is used forty-six times. By 1819, when it appears in Hazlitt's essay "Wit and Humor," "wit" is a pejorative that denotes something artificial.

Hazlitt's essay begins: "Man is the only animal that laughs and weeps; for he is the only animal that is struck with the difference between what things are, and what they ought to be." This difference, in the eyes of the Romantic poets, widened at an accelerating pace during the latter part of the eighteenth century as England's economy shifted from an agrarian to an industrial base, and great technological advances improved life for the few and—as the poor could no longer live by farming and migrated to the cities—wreaked even more misery than usual on the many. In 1798, the year *Lyrical Ballads* first appeared, Thomas Malthus argued in his *Essay on the Principle* that poverty was the result of overpopulation and the best and simplest way to deal with the poor was to let them die off as quickly as possible, without the interference of organized charity. As the modernist revolution was a right-wing coup, the Romantics were of the left; and, like the Bolshevik Revolution, the French Revolution raised great hopes among the left for social justice and then shattered them. In the aftermath, the English Romantics, through various forms of exile, withdrew from society, but society had already withdrawn from them. Dryden and Pope could at least regard themselves as public poets whose audience was the elite of society. If Pope had only 575 subscriptions to his *Iliad,* he could boast with only some exaggeration that they included "almost all the distinguished names of Quality or Learning in the Nation." Whatever immediate, tangible social role the poet had in England after the Middle Ages he certainly no longer had by 1800, but what most clearly distinguishes the Romantic poet from his predecessors is his giving up the idea of one. Contrast Dryden's "I confess my chief endeavors are to delight the age I live in" to Keats's "I never wrote one single line of Poetry with the least shadow of public thought." For Shelley, the poet is "a nightingale who sits in darkness and sings to cheer his own solitude with sweet sounds," a nightingale who doubles, perhaps on the dayshift, as "an unacknowledged legislator of the world." Appropriately enough, the "Defence of Poetry" in which this phrase appears was not only ignored during Shelley's lifetime, it wasn't even published until almost twenty years after his death. As a legislator of the world, he was certainly unacknowledged.

As Shelley's phrase indicates, the Romantic poets replaced the idea of the poet who promotes good by teaching virtue and moving his fellow citizens toward it with a considerably less modest and more abstract idea of his social role. This is how Wordsworth put it in the 1800 preface to *Lyrical Ballads:*

> In spite of the difference of soil and climate, of language and manners, of laws and customs: in spite of things gone silently out of mind, and things violently destroyed; the Poet binds together by passion and knowledge the vast empire of human society, as it is spread over the whole earth, and over all time.

What Wordsworth did here is as ingenious and disfiguring as Sidney's transmutation of Plato. By imagining the audience to be permanent and universal instead of immediate and particular, Wordsworth awards the poet a larger, lasting, more important role in "the vast empire of human society" (far beyond England in 1800), the actual nonreaders who would rather quaff Guinness in the local pub be damned. What's given up, besides the contact and corrective of a real audience, is the poet's role as citizen. By putting himself above the local and immediate, the Romantic poet becomes alien and possibly subversive. In this regard, Shelley's reading of Plato is more faithful than Sidney's. In his isolation, and with a self-projected, imagined audience, the poet also acquires enormous potential for solipsism and self-aggrandizement (which since has been fully realized as the primary occupational hazard).

The last part of Wordsworth's sentence is worth focusing on: "The Poet binds together by passion and knowledge the vast empire of human society, as it is spread over the whole earth, and over all time." Whereas Sidney is speaking literally and practically when he says the social function of poetry is "to teacheth and moveth to virtue,"

Wordsworth's use of language here is terrifically figurative: the audience itself is imagined as all Humanity (capital H), and this Humanity is somehow metaphorically bound together by the poet's passion and knowledge. This seems pretty abstract now, and, although we may have some notion of what Wordsworth is talking about (since we work within the realm of his assumptions), it's an idea that became impossible to swallow after the reports of Nazi concentration camp directors reading Goethe and listening to Beethoven as the day's allotment of Jews was being gassed. In our century, art by itself does not necessarily "humanize"; even if it's a humanizing force, it has shown itself to be impotent against much more powerful forces of economics, technology, and history.

Wordsworth certainly believed that civilization was, in Pound's term, a "botch": the main source of evil, brutality, and corruption of the human spirit. And he also believed poetry could do something about it:

> A multitude of causes, unknown to former times, are now acting
> with a combined force to blunt the discriminating powers of the
> mind, and, unfitting it for all voluntary exertion, to reduce it
> to a state of almost savage torpor. The most effective of these
> causes are the great national events which are daily taking place,
> and the increasing accumulation of men in cities, where the uni-
> formity of their occupations produces a craving for extraordinary
> incident which the rapid communication of intelligence hourly
> gratifies . . . ; reflecting upon the magnitude of the general evil, I
> should be oppressed with no dishonourable melancholy, had I not
> a deep impression of certain inherent and indestructible qualities
> of the human mind, and likewise of certain powers in the great
> and permanent objects that act upon it, which are equally inher-
> ent and indestructible.

These "great and permanent objects that act upon" the mind are, for Wordsworth, the objects of Nature, and the "inherent and indestructible qualities of the human mind" are essentially two: memory and imagination. Most poetry since Wordsworth has dramatized possible interactions of the social and natural world with these two qualities of the mind, and our expectation in reading a poem is still that they will come into play. But for Wordsworth the interaction of memory and imagination with Nature has behind it a coherent moral force, a very definite idea of the poet's social function: namely, if people are re-educated according to Nature and the "inherent and indestructible qualities of the human mind," society will get itself back on the right path. The idea comes from Rousseau, whom Wordsworth read while living in France in the early 1790s. It's this idea, not some disembodied aesthetic, that made Wordsworth think poems should be "a man speaking to men . . . in language really used by men."

In the same essay in which Wordsworth asserts that "the Poet binds together . . . the vast empire of human society," having imagined the grandest audience out of the thinnest air, he admits that, in fact, the poet's "own feelings are his stay and support." The whole drama of the poet's relationship to his audience becomes internalized in the theater of the poet's own mind—what Keats charitably called "the Wordsworthian or egotistical sublime." Yet, in that theater, Words-worth, no less than Sidney, wrote for an audience, and would not have conceded that his ideas contain the seeds of the *poète maudit*, the poet's final isolation from society, and the movement of art for art's sake that influenced the young Yeats. "What is the Character of the Poet?" is the question most frequently and urgently asked in Roman-tic poetics, because, in fact, what sort of person could possibly bind "together by passion and knowledge the vast empire of human soci-ety" against "the magnitude of general evil" and the destructive forces of civilization and still be his own "stay and support"? No wonder Shelley fell upon the thorns of life and bled.

As Auden says, for the Romantics, "To become a great poet was to become not only superior to other poets but superior to all other men." This pathetic self-delusion, one of our less happy inheritances from the Romantics, probably found its purest avatar in Pound. The elevation of art and the artist ("the unacknowledged legislators of the world") is only a compensation for his diminished social role, the other side of the coin to Rocky's "What do you want me to do? Stay at home all day and write *poems?*" In the absence of a living, breathing audience, in the presence of a grandiose, imagined one, the poet's self-aggrandizement is a natural trap. Romantic Ego and Romantic Agony are born of the same germ. The Great Man laboring mightily in solitude to produce Masterworks, the Genius with infinite energy and unstoppable will, as well as the self-destructive, drunk, deranged young poet, are mythic figures of our culture, to which too many poets have sacrificed themselves and their lives and everyone they loved. That poets are mythic figures may also explain the inevitably greater interest in their biographies after they are dead than in their poetry while they are alive, especially if they lived chaotic lives culminating in suicide. In 1765, Samuel Johnson said confidently that "all claim to poetical honours" must be decided by "the common sense of readers"; less than twenty years later, in 1784, Jeremy Bentham, who was known for his common sense, declared that in terms of social utility "pushpin is as good as poetry." When these two remarks are presented as the major and minor premises, Wordsworth's statement in 1800 that the poet's "own feelings are his stay and support" is the inevitable conclusion of the syllogism.

Walt Whitman read the Romantics carefully, no doubt including the preface to *Lyrical Ballads*. It's by now old news that this most insistently unliterary of poets put in many library hours of literary study, especially in the early 1850s, in preparation for his great, self-appointed task. The task was exactly what Wordsworth had named as the poet's function, only "the vast empire" Whitman hoped to bind together by his passion and knowledge was actual and specific: the vast empire of "these United States." Through *Leaves of Grass*, Whitman intended literally to "inaugurate a religion" in which the poet would be the new priest directing not only the cultural life but also, through his spiritual guidance, the political and social affairs of the burgeoning young nation. In the 1855 preface to *Leaves of Grass*, he wrote:

> Of all nations the United States with veins full of poetical stuff
> most needs poets and will doubtless have the greatest and use
> them the greatest. Their Presidents shall not be their common
> referee so much as their poets shall.

And:

> There will soon be no more priests. Their work is done. They may
> wait awhile . . . perhaps a generation or two . . . dropping off by
> degrees. A superior breed shall take their place . . . the gangs of
> kosmos and prophets en masse shall take their place. A new order
> shall arise and they shall be the priests of man, and every man
> shall be his own priest.

And:

> The greatest poet hardly knows pettiness or triviality. If he
> breathes into any thing that was before thought small it dilates
> with the grandeur and life of the universe. He is a seer . . . he is
> individual . . . he is complete in himself . . . The others are as good
> as he, only he sees it and they do not.

Despite his superior eyesight, Whitman's poet is not superior to his
fellow citizens. He "sees health for himself in being one of the mass."
Though Whitman's great audience of initiates must also be imagined
at first, he most certainly intends for it to become real and present. It
is a nation, not an abstraction. He could and did go out and mingle
in it, even if it wasn't aware of him. Although he knew from the start
that the task would be difficult, he never intended that his "own feelings" would have to be "his stay and support." The last sentence of
the 1855 preface is: "The proof of the poet is that his Country absorbs
him as affectionately as he has absorbed it."

This was Whitman's ambition and his hope, and, despite such
grandeur, the poet would retain his citizenship, like Sidney's moral
instructor or the Greek craftsman-poet. In one bold stroke (there has
never been one bolder in the history of literature), Whitman at-
tempted to swoop up all past figures of the poet and carry them into
the limitless future on the waves of his great rolling lines. These figures would become just part of the multitude contained in the poem's
enormous "I." It may have been his research into the origins of poetry
that led Whitman to print the first edition of *Leaves of Grass* anonymously, with only an unidentified picture on the frontispiece of himself with an open collar: an outdoors man, virile and healthy, the ideal

democrat, a "rough" who takes off his hat to no one and looks everybody square in the eye. This was the new poet, the midcentury American version of the shaman-priest. The poem's continuous present represented a return to the mythic past (*in illo tempore*), a spiritualization of the daily world, an "ultimate vivification to facts, to science, and to common lives" without which "life itself" is "finally in vain."

The daily world of the 1850s was all expansion and possibility, very much like *Leaves of Grass* itself. The spirit of Manifest Destiny was in the air, and it suffused both the content and style of the popular orator's silver-tongued magniloquence. Boorstin says:

> Orations were a form of entertainment. In new towns . . . the spellbinding stump orator was a Nineteenth Century version of the bard, troubadour, or minnesinger. . . . On a historic occasion . . . sharing the orator's words was itself an act of community. Municipal authorities . . . would designate their official orator for each occasion.

By absorbing the orator's spirit, *Leaves of Grass* might also absorb the orator's social role. After the Indians were pushed out, and sometimes before, towns further and further west sprang up with amazing rapidity out of nothing. The first building (or tent) to go up often housed a printing press that would announce the existence of a booming town and the golden opportunities to be found. The idea of the limitless future transformed the present in every aspect of American life, at least among white men. Mexico had been invaded for one reason only, and almost no one pretended otherwise: with all this land from Maine to California, and the wealth it represented, everyone wanted more. Whitman cheered the Mexican War. The town for which he was the booster, for which he mixed "visions and prophecies with current and negotiable realities," was a nation that he envisaged occupying the whole North American continent, plus Cuba, from the North pole to the equator.

But Whitman's first political concern was not the expansion of the states but their union. The threat of "the Secession War," as he always called it, tinged the atmosphere; in the 1850s, it was already a war of words, and represented the only significant threat to this potentially great nation of his. The "United States," in common usage, was a plural noun. Unlike now, each state was independent and part of the federal union by virtue of consent as much as law. Virtually no one, including Abraham Lincoln, questioned states' sovereignty and right to govern. In this context, the idea of Whitman's poem, and even what he believed it could accomplish in terms of actual political effects, seems almost plausible:

> I listened to the Phantom by Ontario's shore,
> I heard the voice arising demanding bards,
> By them all native and grand, by them alone can these States be
>   fused into the compact organism of a Nation.
>
>   ("By Blue Ontario's Shore")

Whitman certainly knew he had no audience. He wasn't just the author of his poem, he was its publisher and, in part, its printer. But exactly as a booster paper could create a town, a poem might create an audience, even a whole nation:

> A few first-class poets, philosophers and authors, have substantially settled and given status to the entire religion, education, law, sociology, etc. of the hitherto civilized world, by tingeing and often, *creating* the atmosphere out of which they have arisen. (my italics)

This is an idea he probably first discovered in Emerson, who told an audience at Harvard in 1833: "We have listened too long to the courtly muses of Europe. . . . If the single man plant himself indomitably on his instincts, and there abide, the huge world will come round to him. . . . A nation of men will for the first time exist." Being a democrat, not a great but "feudal" poet like Shakespeare or Milton (such was Whitman's characterization of them), Whitman sought his audience by trying to derive "that average quality of the American bulk, the people, and getting back to it again." This meant that "the idea of beauty" would "need to be radically changed." The poet's subject would again be the tribe, "the best thoughts" of "mechanics" and "farmers" that "wait unspoken, impatient to be put in shape." "Every day," he wrote to Emerson in 1856, "I go among the people of Manhattan Island, Brooklyn, and other cities, and among the young men, to discover the spirit of them, and to refresh myself."

Whitman's taste for fraternizing with wagon drivers, steamboat captains, and soldiers surely preceded any use he might make of it, but there's no doubt that the great ruddy spirit, good cheer, friendliness, and what he called "amativeness" and "animal magnetism" were also part of his self-creation. Despite the purposely scanty evidence Whitman left us, it tells the story of the willed transformation of Walter Whitman Jr., reporter and poetaster, into Walt Whitman, kosmos and prophet en masse, and of the poignant disparity between the grand vision and lonely life. *Leaves of Grass* was intended to create not only an audience and a nation but also its author. It was a Bible and an alchemical book. Whitman literally gave his life to it or, more accurately, to the idea it represented, and the whole enterprise, even with an intervening century of anything but reasons for optimism, still touches us. Whitman's absolute passion lives in the poem, in moments of beautifully rendered detail and of brilliant lightning movements between lines and stanzas, and still makes *Leaves of Grass* (despite its braggadocio, bad judgment, repetitiousness, and failed intention) an exhilarating, heartbreaking experience each time through.

> I depart as air. . . . I shake my white locks at the runaway sun,
> I effuse my flesh in eddies and drift it in lacy jags.
>
> I bequeath myself to the dirt to grow from the grass I love,
> If you want me again look for me under your bootsoles.

As Whitman grew older, he more often characterized the force of his poem as a religious force. In the preface to the 1872 edition, shortly before the massive attack of paralysis that would make him an invalid, he wrote:

> As there can be, in my opinion, no sane and complete personality, nor any grand and elastic nationality, without the stock element of religion imbuing all the other elements, (like heat in chemistry, invisible itself, but the life of all visible life,) so there can be no poetry worthy the name without that element behind all.

Putting aside sanity and "nationality," and thinking only of what spirit is needed to fuel a lifetime of poetry, it's a statement for poets even now to dismiss at their hazard or, at least, at a hazard to their work. Whitman's legacy is what John Updike calls "a totem-image . . . a kind of Excalibur that none but the pure of heart can seize and wield." Besides the religious passion that required a complete commitment to the great and grand (God or Democracy or, as Updike calls it, "Egotheism"), Whitman's poetry is made of and by no ordinary, everyday person, but by a poet who, in Yeats's words, is "never the bundle of accidence and incoherence that sits down to breakfast; he has been reborn as an idea, something intended, complete." Although the texture and material of Whitman's poetry was daily life, his focusing lens was the result of a self-transformation that couldn't be faked and would now be grandiose, anachronistic, misconceived, and willfully blind. We already know, thanks to Whitman, what waits at the end of this path. As a stylistic influence for poets writing in English, Whitman has been deadly. As a moral influence, the lessons of his miserable life, impenetrable personality, and sheer uniqueness loom powerfully. All the ersatz Whitmans that have come since (Vachel Lindsay, for instance) seem pathetic, and the many poets who have used and continued to use his rhetoric for the sake of producing what sounds like poetry have missed the point entirely:

> It is not on *Leaves of Grass* distinctively as literature, or a specimen thereof, that I feel to dwell, or advance claims. No one will get at my verses who insists upon viewing them as a literary performance, or attempt at such performance, or as aiming merely toward art and aestheticism.

Without an absolute belief in Whitman's social program (impossible now for anyone remotely sane), the style is an empty shell.

The most popular poet in England during Whitman's day was not Tennyson (even given the relatively large audience for a serious poet that he had), but John Keble, whose religious verses, *The Christian Year,* had sold 379,000 copies by 1873. It's Keble's audience, not Tennyson's (or Longfellow's)—or not only Tennyson's and Longfellow's—that Whitman was after, although his ambition obviously did not include the agreeable expression of conventional pieties, but of sentiments that Emily Dickinson, apparently never to read *Leaves of Grass* herself, reported that she heard were "disgraceful," expressed in a manner that the young Henry James, reviewing *Drum-Taps,* said was "an offence against art." This manner and style Whitman decided on in advance. For all his belief in the ineffable, the wordless, and the wisdom of the body, it's remarkable how conscious a designer he was. The few poems in the final edition of *Leaves of Grass* in rhyme and meter (including the anthology chestnut "Captain! My Captain!") show how smart he was to adopt the long cadenced lines of the King James Bible as his prosody. There is no more extreme example of a preconceived idea of the audience and of the social function of a poem determining its whole character. Despite his famous pleasure in contradicting himself, this idea is consistent from the beginning (and before the beginning) to the end. In his earlier notebooks, he wrote these "Rules for Composition":

> A perfectly transparent, plate-glassy style, artless, with no ornaments, or attempt at ornaments. . . .
> Take no illustrations whatever from any ancients or classics. . . . Make no mention or allusion to them whatever except as they relate to the new present things. . . .
> Clearness, simplicity, no twistified or foggy sentences, at all— the most translucid clearness without variation.
> Common idioms and phrases—Yankeeisms and vulgarism— cant expressions when very pat only.

Such consistency over a lifetime is usually the result of will, and of a willful resistance to change, and this brings out the shadow of Whitman's bright spirit in the same way his "grand and elastic nationality" looks less sweetly naive when one remembers the genocide of the Indians he was willing to accept in payment for it. His relentless maintenance of his persona, even (I should say, *especially*) among his intimates and devotees, was not accomplished without loss either to himself or to his poetry. In "A Backward Glance O'er Travell'd Roads," the afterword to the so-called Deathbed Edition of 1888, Whitman says in valediction: "The best comfort of the whole business (after a small band of the dearest friends and upholders . . . [)] is that . . . I have had my say entirely my own way." Small comfort that was, particularly against the backdrop of his initial, grand ambitions.

Whitman never reprinted the original 1855 preface but finally included in his *Collected Prose* what Justin Kaplan called "a bobtailed and emasculated version"—another instance of Whitman's careful, useless attention to his image. Juxtaposing that original version against "A Backward Glance O'er Travell'd Roads" poignantly illustrates his vain hope of returning the poet to his central position in the tribe. At the beginning, Whitman set the criterion of his success: "that his country absorbs him as affectionately as he has absorbed it." At the end, he admits "I have not gain'd the acceptance of my own time, but have fallen back on fond dreams of the future."

The future was always a crucial ingredient in Whitman's vision, as it is in all apocalyptic visions, but finally the themes he had reiterated thousands of times in his poetry, essays, letters, and conversations are stated with unusual quietness. In his "fond dreams of the future" he still (at least publicly) believed that there might "arise a race of poets varied, yet one in soul—not only poets, and of the best, but newer, larger prophets—larger than Judea's, and more passionate—to melt and penetrate these woes, as shafts of light the darkness." But as far as *Leaves of Grass* was concerned, he had to concede his vision had been a chimera. He wrote in an anonymous review of himself that his poems "have fallen stillborn in this country. They have been met, and are met today, with the determined denial, disgust, and scorn of orthodox American authors, publishers, and editors, and in a pecuniary and worldly sense, have certainly wrecked the life of their author." Walt Whitman, the cheerful, white-bearded "good gray poet" Walter Whitman Jr. created to write *Leaves of Grass,* would never have published this under his own signature, but it gives us a heartbreakingly vivid picture of the person who had to live the good gray poet's life.

Asked for his opinion of Whitman's poetry, Wallace Stevens wrote, "It seems to me . . . that Whitman is disintegrating as the world, of which he made himself a part, disintegrates." On another occasion, he equated Whitman with a poetaster, Joachim Miller, and called him a "poseur." These remarks say more about Stevens than they do about Whitman, but none of the modernist poets—with the exceptions of Williams and Pound, who compared Whitman to a "pigheaded father"—had much interest in Whitman's poetry, his enterprise, or its failure. After the first World War, the world seemed to be "disintegrating." "Poets in our civilization, as it exists at present, must be difficult," Eliot wrote—a sentence that Philip Larkin angrily said "gave the modernist poetry movement its charter." Just as Whitman's biblical cadences and "perfectly transparent, plate-glassy style" were designed to reach as many people as possible, Eliot's "difficult" style of juxtaposition, allusion, and disjointed syntax was meant to address, as he said, "the one perfectly intelligent reader who does not exist."

Ironically, Eliot had many more readers in his lifetime than Whitman had in his, but if Whitman's idea of his audience predetermined his idea of his poetic style, Eliot's ideas were probably acquired concurrently. At the Harvard University that Eliot and Stevens attended, Laforgue's dandyism and the affectations of the *poète maudit* were *de rigueur* for the campus *literati*. It was generally assumed that poetry was a "superior entertainment," as Eliot later called it, for superior men. And the larger world for Eliot, as for the *symbolistes*, was a "brutal mirage." This is the world that appears in *The Waste Land*, the poem that for Pound was "the culmination of our movement." Eliot's earlier poetic strategies and ideas about poetry are defensive—defensive of the poet's high cultural importance in the world that actually ignores him. Although Eliot took the phrasings of his ideas from many different sources, the tenor of his ideas comes straight out of Romantic poetics, the Shelley he despised as well as the Coleridge he admired.

Obviously, the literary atmosphere has changed greatly since *The Sacred Wood* and *The Waste Land* and the halcyon days of Scofield Thayer's *The Dial,* but the cultural position of poetry has not. In the United States, the difference between the sales of five thousand copies of a volume of poems, which is unusually high, and fifty thousand copies, which is almost unheard of, is the difference between minute fractions of one percent of the population. Every poet alive has felt the consequences of this fact in many forms—the most basic being that, unlike painters or prose writers, a poet can never even hope to live from what he produces and therefore must continually do other things to buy time to write. TV and movies and advertising "teach" and "delight" the citizenry, not poetry. Whether or not Sidney would have recognized what they teach as virtue, they most definitely do teach the materialist values of the culture, the values of corporate capitalism.

Poets teach, too, but in the classroom. "Academic poetry," after World War II, was initially a descriptive, not a pejorative, term. Modest as it may seem, classroom teaching—not writing—is now the poet's main social utility. Just as it was for Dryden and Pope, the poet's social usefulness is the source of his livelihood, and the source of his livelihood has at least that much power to enforce aesthetic values. The genteel tradition that has forever confused the beautiful and the agreeable took root in American universities at their inception and has flourished there ever since in conservative political atmospheres. Further, as Larkin said, "the emergence of English literature as an academic subject" led to a "consequent demand for a kind of poetry that needed elucidation." These two influences by themselves are enough to create the pressure for a poetic style that values ingenuity over profundity, nicety of expression over passion, restraint over candor, and complication—even opacity—over simplicity. Whatever else might be said about the differences in their poetry, this explains the common academic approval of James Merrill and John Ashbery and the styles of a number of younger poets who naturally, and most often unconsciously, gravitate toward the source of their livelihood.

But the university is an employer of teachers, not a patron of artists. The poet's dependence on the university is more complex and various, and, as an economic source, the university is infinitesimal compared either to the relative wealth and power of the Church in Bellini's Venice or to the total economic resources available in the United States. A poet can survive on the fringes of the academy and outside of it if he has a marketable skill. Paradoxically, by virtue of the material worthlessness of his product, the poet has a unique chance to become a free agent with a free imagination. He doesn't have to tack on happy endings or direct his message to urban dwellers between the ages of thirty-four and thirty-nine who make over a hundred thousand dollars per year. Knowing how important it is to have "worthless" art in a market-driven economy, some foundations, endowments, and universities do not want the poet starved into extinction, although the poets they choose to support are not likely to be the ones who challenge the ideological premises by which they themselves exist. A result of this freedom is a dizzying proliferation of poetic styles and almost no commonality of taste, which unhappily makes critical judgment seem arbitrary, reputations disproportionate, and awards meaningless. According to an ancient anecdote retold by Pliny, Polykleitos won an important sculpture contest in Athens because in the voting all the other sculptors picked him second, after themselves. By contrast, ten randomly chosen American poets picking their ten most esteemed contemporaries would probably result in a list of almost a hundred names. Poets cluster around writing programs and magazines, all with circulations of fifteen thousand or less, usually much less, and, as a consequence, contemporary poetry is glutted by the "coterie writing" that Yeats warned against. The danger of writing for a small group is tunnel vision, mistaking the "accidental and temporary" for the essential and permanent. For Wordsworth, "pleasure" was "the grand elementary principle." And for Coleridge, the "origin and object" of poetry is "pleasurable excitement": "Pleasure is the magic circle out of which the poet dare not tread." But without an audience at large, and with, at best, a specialized audience of academics and other poets who agree on almost nothing, how is a poet to judge what constitutes "pleasure," much less what is essential and permanent?

Poets themselves are often blamed for this situation, but it's only a reflection of the much-documented fragmentation of the culture as a whole. As Whitman demonstrated once and for all, the role of the poet in his culture is far beyond his individual desire and control. Even if by a miraculous conjunction of the stars, a real poet were to sell a million copies of his or her books, a TV show with only a million viewers is off the air the next day. And there are many television shows: in the average home with cable, fifty-eight hours of them each week.

Simonides of Ceos, said to be the inventor of the mnemonic art, is also said to be the first poet to receive payment for his work. Enduring qualities of narrative and style—the memorable story, palpable detail, and powerful rhythm—made poetry the preserver of crucial information and cultural wisdom and thereby socially important and economically valuable. But from the beginning, memory had another aspect as well. As Gilbert Murray said, memory was "'the waker of longing,' the enchantress who turns the common to the heavenly and fills men's eyes with tears because the things that are now past were so beautiful." Mnemosyne, the goddess of Memory, was the mother of the Muses, but she was also the daughter of Uranus and Gaea (Heaven and Earth), a Titan, one of the oldest order, born before the reign of the gods of Olympus. In this aspect, memory seems no less a part of poetry today than it was in ancient Greece, and the enduring qualities that made poetry memorable and "the waker of longing" are no less effective now than they ever were. For Milton, these qualities were three: poems should be "simple, sensuous, and passionate." In the same lecture in which he talks about the "magic circle of pleasure," Coleridge approves Milton's three qualities as a definition of poetry and adds: "Had these three words only been properly understood by, and present in the minds of, general readers . . . a library of false poetry would have been precluded or still-born."

It is a truism that, at each moment of history, the world has never existed quite like that before. Sidney, Wordsworth, Whitman, and Pound, in their poems and essays, all expressed a belief that their cultural moments were a special case. But, even with this caveat, it seems that the United States in the year 2000 marks a unique historical moment. Besides the capacity for nuclear annihilation and the destruction of the natural world that continues almost invisibly through various forms of chemical pollution, and the capacity to alter the human body genetically, we are now at the beginning of a time when language is neither the only nor always the most efficient means of communication and preservation of information, ideas, and feelings. "Speech alone has rendered man human," said Herder in the eighteenth century, and language certainly made the inheritance of tradition and the evolution and spreading of cultures possible. The invention of movable type expanded and accelerated information storage so that human memory began to exist, in a sense, outside the body. This process is now being accelerated again at the speed of light. No one knows what the long-term effects of this technology will be, any more than they knew that unchecked burning of fossil fuel would eventually destroy the ozone layer and make the earth a desert. It may even make us all into nicer people alone in our houses with our user-friendly machines. In any case, in this historical moment poetry seems both more anachronistic and more important as a custodian of time, a preserver of bodily memory in its rudimentary sense, the one million years of humanity and three billion years of life of the earth. From this perspective, it's possible to see poetry as not just the product of individuals writing individual poems about individual experience. Heinrich Zimmer, in *The King and the Corpse,* says of storytellers in ancient India: "Each poet adds something of the substance of his own imagination, and the seeds are nourished back to life." Against our culturally acquired way of looking at the world, it may be paradoxically useful now to poets to see poetry also as a communal enterprise. The alternative was put succinctly by Wordsworth: "Every author, as far as he is great and at the same time original, has had the task of creating the taste by which he is to be enjoyed." *Great, original, creating the taste:* these terms belong not only to our literary assumptions but also to a capitalist mythology of individual survival and dominance, as if all human beings were not totally bound up with one another and all life on earth. It's the same mythology that makes the idea of writing poetry an absurdity to Rocky and to a culture that measures the quality of life in money and status. It seems that there have been enough examples to show that these assumptions are inherently self-destructive and self-defeating. For a poet, given his lack of audience and social role, they breed humiliation, grandiosity, isolation, and bitterness. They have no necessary connection to poetry. They present the shortest view, of a set of Western countries, of a small percentage of the world's population, during a brief period of history. "It's what the tribe feels that is sacred": Our culture's elevation of the individualism and selfishness in its many forms does not by any means represent an absolute truth, psychological or moral.

Wonderful poetry has been written out of the attempt to survive in isolation—Hopkins's Terrible Sonnets, Edwin Arlington Robinson's dramatic lyrics, Stevens's late poetry written "not for an audience" but as "one of the sanctions of life"—but for all its intensity this poetry cannot communicate "the bloom of shared pleasure" that comes from collective emotions fundamental to human experience and therefore to art. "The bloom of shared pleasure" is Eudora Welty's phrase. She uses it to describe Jane Austen's novels, which Austen was not initially able to publish, but read chapter by chapter to her family. This is what an audience can do. It can make the writer feel the human community that shares his love of what Stanley Kunitz calls "the sacred fire," a feeling that can change the character of the writing itself. There need be no dominance involved in this relationship, and it can provide an emotional support that between two people is an element of love. As Gilbert Murray said, this spirit and this impulse—even when writing about the most internal, personal subjects—has existed in poetry since the beginning:

> Love, Strife, Death, and that which is beyond Death. Those are, it would seem, definitely the four themes about which our earliest bards sang, and, when singing was not enough to express all their stress of emotion, yearned and reached out their arms amid the dancers.

A NOTE ON FORM

The modernist distrust of received forms (or, more precisely, Pound's and Eliot's distrust of them during their Imagist phase) derives from the conviction that they allow only certain kinds of poems to be written, the kinds of poems that are the monuments of English literature but had fallen into decadence at the beginning of the twentieth century. The advantage of received forms is nonetheless still obvious: they insist that there be some interaction of the formal properties of the words used, even if that insistence is as gentle as blank verse's ten-syllable pattern of predominantly alternate stress. Therefore, theoretically at least, they push the poem away from prose cut into lines, and tend to influence a slight jarring into new meaning. Their disadvantage, from our vantage in literary history, is even more obvious: even if English had the syntactical flexibility, relatively few vowel sounds, and rhyming suffixes of inflected languages like Italian or Russian, received forms still could not accommodate all formal impulses; or—to see it from another angle, the angle of the poem's generation—the interaction of formal properties of words in any language and especially English is too rich and various to be standardized. In Pound's view (about 1912), received forms promoted bad writing because they didn't allow the writer to say what he would, "in the stress of some emotion, actually say." As with the Romantics, most of the complicated formal innovations of the modernists were based on the simple need to reform poetic diction, to bring it closer to the vitality of speech. Yeats, partially due to Pound's influence, changed his diction, but rhyme and meter were to him essential aids to composition; he could write no poetry without traditional verse forms: "Ancient salt," he said, "is the best packing."

Frost was surely right in thinking free verse is a contradiction in terms. As Delmore Schwartz said of Williams's prosodic notion of a variable foot, it's like an elastic inch. Good "free verse" is really formal improvisation. The words interconnect and interact formally every bit as thoroughly as in the strictest sonnet. The difference is that no pattern of interaction, however partial, is set at the beginning—to allow for a greater richness of formal interaction, not a lesser, to allow (theoretically) for an even greater instrumentality of the language. The form of the poem is the way the poem tells the poet what it wants to be. Once the poet has absorbed this way of feeling language and responding to its emerging form-in-verse, he may stand as a kind of censor, rejecting the impulses that aren't *right* in every possible way—in meaning as well as sound and arrangement. Auden, thinking mostly about content, wanted to extend the Censor to a Censorate that included "a sensitive only child, a practical housewife, a logician, a monk, an irreverent buffoon and even, perhaps, hated by all the others and returning their dislike, a brutal, foul-mouthed drill sergeant who considers all poetry rubbish." One might also include a decent professional musician or at least a piano tuner, someone with a trained ear. A poet may begin writing poems as program notes to his personality, and maybe they should always retain that early ardor of self-expression, but the best poets care about the poem as a made thing as much as about what it says, and to them the two are as inseparable as a word from its sound.

Whether we are aware of it or not, the formal properties of language make their own complex patterns that are followed and, to some extent, fulfilled in all language usage, even in discursive prose. The most scholarly article, researched and outlined in advance, will probably come out with a few surprises in it for the writer. Writing at the top of page one, he can't predict the exact words he will use at the bottom of page two. As E. M. Forster has the old lady in *Howard's End* exclaim, "How can I know what I think until I see what I say?" This is one of the greatest joys of writing. As Frost put it, "The wonder of unexpected supply keeps growing." But for most writers it's the source of no end of fretting as well.

A poet, released from many of the responsibilities of the scholar, in the end has others that are more onerous. Frost said, "The poem begins in delight and ends in wisdom." That is a large demand. On another occasion, Frost put the same formula in different terms: "Poetry begins in trivial metaphors, pretty metaphors, 'grace' metaphors, and goes on to the profoundest thinking that we have." Like many of Frost's remarks about poetry, both of these emphasize the writing as an act of discovery, but "the profoundest thinking that we have" *is* metaphorical thinking and it is taking place as soon as the poem begins. The act of making metaphor is inherent in the linguistic act, as well as in all of our most important operations of mind. The foundation blocks of science are metaphors (as in the term "foundation blocks"): chemical "bonding," the properties of light as "waves" and "particles," the "conscious" and "unconscious" (*unbewusst,* which also translates as "unaware, involuntary, instinctive"— a term that didn't exist in any language until it was coined by German Romantics in the eighteenth century). The words we use are the results of the confluence of historical currents ("currents"—we can hardly speak without metaphor). Yet we act as if these words refer to real things because of our habit of using language-as-linkage, and we even use them to explain metaphor itself when in fact they are themselves metaphors.

In this way, language can become self-referential and jargon-ridden. Too much inbreeding causes it to lose vitality. The significance of metaphor, Stevens argued in *The Necessary Angel,* always derives from its reference to reality. The root of metaphor—from Greek *meta-pherein*—means "carry over" or "bear across," and implies a conceptual movement, a translation from wordlessness into words. Blake exhorted us to "cleanse the doors of perception": not the windows, the doors, that which allows exit and entrance. Physiologically, we see more with our brain than with our eyes, according to expectation and habituation; the same might be said of metaphorical seeing with the brain of cultural expectation and linguistic habit. Blake, Dickinson, Stevens, to cite only three examples among many other poets of every language and culture, took it as their explicit purpose to challenge these habits and make something compellingly beautiful, to articulate a more vital way of being and seeing than those that dominated their historical moments. For none of these three poets was this a matter of choice. Since they depended on what they learned through language-arranged-in-verse, their formal discoveries were for each of them life-sustaining.

"No surprise for the writer, no surprise for the reader" (Frost, again): readers also want the poem to change their way of seeing. Yet, for the sake of survival, the brain programs itself to limit vision, in both senses. One of the symptoms of schizophrenia is sensory over-load; the brain can't process all the data presented to it by the body. The brain functions properly more by exclusion than inclusion—like art, through a selection and presentation of detail. But there always remains the central human and aesthetic question about *what* is being excluded. As Auden said, "A poem may fail in two ways: it may ex-clude too much (banality), or attempt to embody more than one community at once (disorder)."

If language arose out of the need to communicate shared tasks in order to survive, then its original function was to exclude from atten-tion what was unimportant to the task at hand, thereby providing an ordering of the experience of the world. That exclusion, which char-acterizes rationality and discursiveness, is also useful to poetry, be-cause it is in the balance between order and inclusion that poems are made. As Stevens said, "The poem must resist the intelligence *almost* successfully." The "blessed rage for order" must win in the end be-cause it is that which allows us to survive. However, if the battle against it—by fate, by human frailty and fragility, by the unconscious and preliterate, by the sound and rhythm of the words—is not a rag-ing battle, the poem will seem to have excluded too much. According to Auden's useful little failure-formula, it will be banal.

But a poem can also bring the previously unknown and unformed to consciousness. It can give it apprehensible shape and form. It can communicate, in the root sense of that word (to make common), as clearly as any other kind of discourse, while it embodies the manifold patterning that marks the preliterate, nonrational modes of the brain.

Poems proceed in two ways at once: in time, sequentially, insofar as the first word is read first, the second word second, and so on; and *in illo tempore*, as a pattern forming as we read the words and formed after we have read them. The latter is indicated by our intuitions of closure—as Yeats said, "The poem comes right with a click like a closing box." We feel a sequence and pattern join and complete itself. So each word must not only promote its own interest, to stir us out of our linguistic habits, but it must also engage us in the manifold pattern emerging. This may be why we are unsatisfied by a string of brilliant images, no matter how amazing or amusing each is in itself, if that's all the poem is; and are at least as unsatisfied by poems whose individual moments are predetermined by an obvious logic, whose pattern seems mechanical or static. We want richness, evocation, connections too various for analysis, much less for codification by prosody. We want to feel the poem as we feel the atmosphere when entering a room where so many things are happening we can't possibly isolate them. There has never been a poet smart enough to do this by himself. The poem does it through the agency of lines, sentences, stanzas, silences, and sounds, through the instrumentality of language used in formal conjunction, not just according to the dictates of logic or narrative or any other principle of organization: conjunction made possible by form. The mode of logic, or discursiveness, is only one mode that a poem may include within it; as Stanley Burnshaw pointed out, there is in poetry an opportunity for "plurality of modes of thought" and "both common and uncommon sense together." The form of poetry gives us a way of thinking beneath and beyond thought that returns much more than we are able to put in: "a momentary stay against confusion," in Frost's fine phrase, embodied in language we may fully experience and most deeply understand.

THE LITERARY DICTATOR

In 1947, the same year Delmore Schwartz dubbed him "The Literary Dictator," T. S. Eliot said of himself that he had "an incapacity for the abstruse, and an interest in poetry that is primarily a technical interest." No poet's self-characterizations hold for a lifetime, much less other poets' characterizations of him, but Eliot's later ones were meant to be straightforward, and, unlikely as it sounds, this one was accurate in both its parts. His "incapacity for the abstruse" showed in his admitted "mishandling of philosophical criticism" in the early thirties, when his royalist political and cultural theories so infected his literary criticism that he concluded, in *After Strange Gods*, that Pound, Lawrence, and Hardy were heretics because of their lack of moral orthodoxy. After the vehemently negative response to *After Strange Gods*, he tried to separate his personal beliefs from his literary interests. He announced in the October 1933 issue of *The Criterion* that he would now approach the "problems of contemporary civilization" as a "moralist," not as an "artist."

But Eliot's cast of mind was always to seek the integration of his thought, to seek ambitious connections among both discrete disciplines and self-conflicts. His ideas, good and bad, issue from a poignant desire for wholeness and coherence. Despite his earlier experience, in his last essays he insists that "moral, religious, and social judgments cannot be wholly excluded" from literary criticism. So by agreeing with R. P. Blackmur (and Eliot himself) that Eliot was at his best as "a technical critic," I don't mean to suggest that larger questions were not on his mind. The opposite is the case: the pressure of large questions gives his technical criticism its force. A description of how a poem works is trivial unless it's infused with an awareness of what the poem is working for, its place in human life. Eliot's career as a critic teaches us the hazards of this awareness, but much more its value when it pervades the practicing poet's point of view conducting, as Eliot put it, his "private poetry workshop" with the poets he most admires. Eliot's best essays invariably penetrate the occasion to the permanent issue inside it: on Yeats (1940) to the character of the poet in general; on Samuel Johnson (1944) to the way the different poetic assumptions of different literary periods always reveal and complement each other.

At the end of his life, Eliot complained about the friendly critics who cited his early ideas as if they represented his current thinking, who represented him by those phrases such as "dissociation of sensibility" and "objective correlative" that had, as he put it, "a truly embarrassing success in the world." By mid-century, at least in literature classes, Eliot's "objective correlative" was as ubiquitous as Freud's popularized terms and probably no better understood. Its definition in "Hamlet and His Problems" certainly invites confusion:

> The only way of expressing emotion in the form of art is by finding an "objective correlative"; in other words, a set of objects, a situation, a chain of events which shall be the formula of that particular emotion; such that when the external facts, which must terminate in sensory experience, are given, the emotion is immediately evoked.

Does this mean the poet first has an emotion, say of love, and then finds some objects, say flowers and trees, to embody it? Before the hundredth time he saw this quoted, Eliot *should* have winced at the distorting oversimplification and pretentious pseudoscientific diction, the worst of his style and temperament—Mr. Eliot, as Virginia Woolf said, "in his *four*-piece suit."

The definition is followed by a discussion of Hamlet's character, but there's no question that "by finding an 'objective correlative'" Eliot meant a way of working for the poet. Along with "intensity," for him the essential quality of poetry was what he described variously as "objectivity," "presentation," and "realization." His own *Poems of 1920* have this quality of emotion held in check, of (as he wrote of Pound's poems in 1919) having "written themselves." In a 1920 lecture entitled "Modern Tendencies in Poetry" published in an Indian magazine called *Shama'a* and never reprinted, he said:

> The poet's "emotion" must always be in such close relation to objects that when he sets the objects before you, you "get" the emotion. He must appeal to your senses. The emotion is the resultant activity of what are ultimately sense-data. . . . The thing is to *cease to feel* the emotion, to *see* it as the objective equivalent for it. . . . You must find the formula for it. We might almost work out the James-Lange theory of emotion for poetry: an emotion *is* the physical equivalent.

If this is clearer than the definition in "Hamlet and His Problems," its source is also less disguised, which may be why he never reprinted the lecture. Eliot took the "objective correlative" from Ford Madox Ford. In *Ezra Pound: His Metric and His Poetry,* published anonymously in 1917, Eliot himself quotes Ford: "Poetry consists in so rendering concrete objects that the emotions produced by the objects shall arise in the reader."

The "objective correlative" may be the grandest larceny in "Hamlet and His Problems," but it isn't the only one. Two pages later Eliot writes:

> The intense feeling, ecstatic or terrible, without an object or exceeding its object, is something which every person of sensibility has known. . . . The artist keeps it alive by the ability to intensify the world to his emotions.

Compare this to the following passage from *Poetry and Religion* (1900) by George Santayana, Eliot's teacher at Harvard: "The poet's art is to a great extent the art of intensifying emotions by assembling the scattered objects that naturally arouse them." This marriage of "objectivity" and "intensity" does represent Eliot's central idea of poetry in *The Sacred Wood*, but now it seems merely curious that Eliot didn't simply credit Santayana and Ford as its source and take as his own work its elaborations, modifications, implications, and applications. Curious but characteristic. He also borrowed the subjects, technique, and even the tone of his early poems from Laforgue, Baudelaire, and others. This habit, this way of writing ("mature poets steal"), indicates the private investment Eliot had in his notions of "Impersonality" and "Tradition" and may explain why these notions are absurdly idealized in his early essays. No one, not even Eliot himself, ever wrote a poem "with a feeling that the whole of the literature of Europe from Homer and within it the whole of literature of his own country has a simultaneous existence and composed a simultaneous order." This notorious line is from "Tradition and the Individual Talent," which Frank Kermode called "arguably Eliot's most influential essay." Its arrogance, pedantry, and exaggeration still seem unfortunate, not only because it spawned a snotty bookishness and willful obscurity in poetry from which we have not fully recovered, but also because poets do use tradition, consciously or not, just as we all do when we use a fork (or chopsticks) or speak or write or think, and the reaction against Eliot among poets has sometimes resulted in the equally impoverishing belief that "traditional" means conservative and unoriginal. William Carlos Williams, among others, was (without exaggeration) obsessed with the pernicious effects of Eliot's influence.

But one positive effect of Eliot's early criticism was to reestablish poetry as an art in a literary atmosphere in which poetry was judged solely by its content, by the "nobility" of the poet's sentiments. In response to the popularity of the imperialism and sentimentality of Noyes, Watson, and Kipling, Eliot argued that a poem must be a thing in itself: "The poem has its own existence, apart from us, it was there before us and will endure after us." He believed, rightly, that a poet must find his way through the boundaries of his ego, the tunnel vision of the merely personal, although that doesn't necessarily mean that "the emotion of art is *im*personal." It does mean, à la Santayana, that the intensity of the poet's personal feelings must be reined and directed by the process of composition:

> It is not the "greatness," the intensity, of the emotions, the components, but the intensity of the artistic process, the pressure, so to speak, under which the fusion takes place, that counts.

In other words, intensity is a quality of the poem as a made thing, and the poet's personal emotions are only part of the material he works with.

By 1941, when the territory was secure, Eliot could apply this idea of intensity to both subject and style:

> We expect to feel, with a great writer, that he *had* to write about the subject he took, and in that way.

This surely extends Santayana's original idea. It articulates an important quality of poetry that you might know but can't quite name, and this is why such remarks are so memorable and were seized to construct a whole new critical vocabulary by both Eliot's generation and the one that followed.

But "intensity" was also an aspect of Eliot's personality and, consistently enough, the one he tried most to conceal. Pound called him "the Possum," a nickname from his Harvard days which he later used, self-ironically, for his *Book of Practical Cats*. And this intensity made objective characterizes the best moments of his poetry. It's what has made readers return to *The Waste Land* even when the whole seemed inchoate, and sent them chasing through the library to try to construct a coherence through allusion guided by notes that Eliot himself in 1956 called "a remarkable exhibition of bogus scholarship." It's what I. A. Richards noticed when he reviewed *The Waste Land* in 1924: "The poem as a whole may elude us, while every fragment as a fragment comes victoriously home." It's a quality of palpability, of some *thing* dredged from a dark place and put before us:

> Who is the third who walks always beside you?
> When I count there are only you and I together

But when I look ahead up the white road
There is always another one walking beside you
Gliding wrapt in a brown mantle, hooded
I do not know whether a man or a woman
—But who is that on the other side of you?

The palpability, drama, and poetic effect of these lines don't depend on their "allusion" to the account of a polar expedition from which Eliot copied them, nor would they if he had taken them from Dante, Ovid, or the Upanishads and given them a footnote.

For Eliot, the marriage of intensity and objectivity is most powerful when the poem's material has "tentacular roots reaching down to the deepest terrors and desires." Eliot was a night roamer. In Boston and London, he would walk the streets fascinated by the transformation of the daytime world, at once obsessed and repelled by sex. Some of his most vivid writing—the woman in the doorway in "Rhapsody on a Windy Night," the pub-closing scene in *The Waste Land*—comes from this experience. His major poems until *Four Quartets* are hallucinatory, pervaded by agonies of guilt and self-loathing, populated by characters and *personae* who live nightmarish lives in a nightmarish world. He said in 1933:

The essential advantage for a poet is not to have a beautiful world with which to deal: it is to be able to see beneath both beauty and ugliness; to see the boredom, and the horror, and the glory.

This passage is taken from one of the Charles Eliot Norton Lectures he delivered at Harvard in the winter of 1932–33 (published as *The Use of Poetry and the Use of Criticism*). When he returned home to England, he refused to see his wife despite her desperate pleadings, and stayed with Frank Morley on his farm. In typically distancing rhetoric, Eliot later recalled the time to Morley as a time "when a man may feel he had come to pieces, and at the same time is standing in the road inspecting the parts, wondering what sort of machine it will make if he can put it together again." Eliot was forty-five, at the first peak of his reputation as a poet and critic. His *Selected Essays* had been welcomed as a major literary event the previous year. In that year

(1932), there were books devoted to his work published in, among
other places, London, Paris, Seattle, Finland, and Peking. Yet, he wrote
to Paul Elmer More, "Pure literary criticism has ceased to interest
me" (the expression of which is *After Strange Gods*). And in 1933, in
another one of his third-person locutions, he confided to Bonamy
Dobree that "he was abandoning the writing of poems" because "he
did not want to repeat himself." His personal life was a shambles.
Vivienne Eliot had been having problems with her "nerves," as it was
then called, since the early twenties:

> "My nerves are bad to-night. Yes, bad. Stay with me.
> "Speak to me. Why do you never speak. Speak.
> "What are you thinking of? What thinking? What?
> "I never know what you are thinking. Think."
>
> I think we are in rats' alley
> Where the dead men lost their bones.

Pound said that being at home for Eliot must have been "like trying
to write in a madhouse."

So in 1941, when Eliot said of Kipling that he "knew something of
the things which are underneath, and of things which are beyond the
frontier," his remark has the saddening authority of his own poetry
and his own life. But even if the underside of the psyche was Eliot's
territory, he realized the material of poetry may also come from memory charged with other feelings:

> I suggest what gives [Chapman's and Seneca's imagery] such in-
> tensity as it has is its saturation . . . with feelings too obscure for
> the authors even to know what they were. And of course only
> a part of an author's imagery comes from his reading. It comes
> from the whole of his sensitive life since early childhood. Why,
> for all of us, out of all we have heard, seen, felt, in a lifetime, do
> certain images recur, charged with emotion, rather than others?
> The song of one bird, the leap of one fish, at a particular place and
> time, the scent of one flower, an old woman on a German moun-
> tain path, six ruffians seen through an open window playing cards
> at a small French railway station where there was a water-mill:

such memories may have symbolic value, but of what we cannot tell, for they come to represent the depths of feeling into which we cannot peer. We might just as well ask why, when we try to recall visually some period of the past, we find in our memory just the few meagre arbitrarily chosen set of snapshots that we do find there, the faded poor souvenirs of passionate moments.

This is one time that Eliot's "we" is not royal. True to his (and Freud's) century, Eliot believed in the nonrational, the "unconscious," as both material for poetry and means of composition. In the body of his essays, he frequently refers to the poet as a vehicle (as well as a maker), the poet's not knowing what he has to say until he says it, his composition as an outpouring, an annihilation, a relief from an intolerable burden; and to the generation of the poem in the "auditory imagination," "a rhythm that brings to birth the idea and the image," the poem shaping itself "in fragments of musical rhythm"; and to the "first voice of the poet" as a voice "speaking to himself, or to no one" at "frontiers of consciousness beyond which words fail but meanings still exist." You don't have to look beyond Eliot's own poems to see how deep are his "tentacular roots." In his criticism, the highest praise is reserved for those poets who look "into a good deal more than the heart . . . into the cerebral cortex, the nervous system, and digestive tracts."

Eliot was also not humorless, with his ironic "Giaconda smile" and lifelong admiration of Groucho Marx. The dustjacket of the first edition of *Old Possum's Book of Practical Cats* sports a caricature of the two of them on roller skates. But there's no doubt that for Eliot the unconscious uncontrolled provoked a primitive terror; hence his politics, his philosophy, and probably also his religion (terror being an excellent foundation for faith). He suffered profound inner conflict between the dayworld and nightworld, the banker's costume at the office (bowlers and Malacca-handled umbrellas) and the madhouse at home, the fastidious manners and the feelings they concealed. Only he himself knew if he ever mended this split in himself, but it is surely reflected in the limits and character of his poems. Eliot could capture the nightworld only in fragments, as in *The Waste Land,*

and could accomplish a sense of wholeness, such as that of *Four Quartets*, only by excluding this material. Eliot the critic would have called it a defect in the character of the artist, rather than a defect of skill. Noting it, some of his critics have pointed to the conflicting presences of his authoritarian, rigid father and his passionate, poeticizing mother; whatever its source, this feeling of irresolution, which was obviously painful, seems also to have caused the extreme need for privacy that made him write and argue for a kind of poetry whose best effects depend on suggestion, a sense of powerful emotion powerfully muted.

In 1933, that crucial year for Eliot in the United States, he gave a talk at Vassar which he began by saying, "My poetry is simple and straightforward." When the audience laughed, he is reported to have reacted with a pained look. Coming from the famous author of *The Waste Land,* the remark must have seemed funny, but had the audience been thinking of Eliot's 1929 essay on Dante they would have known he wasn't joking. For Eliot, Dante was the supreme poet, and *The Divine Comedy* the supreme poem, because of the simplicity of its style and the complexity of its emotional range. Whatever may be the contradictions in his fifty years of criticism, his three Dante essays (1920, 1929, 1950) are a short lesson in the consistency of his ideas and his aspirations for his own poetry. The following is from the last of the three essays, and articulates Eliot's final view of the function of poetry and the social role of the poet. Not accidentally, it's a traditional role—the teacher of his fellow citizens—and incorporates Eliot's own allegiance to the unconscious, his sense of personal conflict, and his desire for Coleridge's "balance or reconcilement of opposite or discordant qualities" in his art and his life. That it's not free of his prejudices and personality, that given the conditions of the world the role of the poet he describes was no less a fantasy in 1950 than it is today, does not make the passage any less poignant, because above all it radiates the passionate love of poetry that permeates Eliot's ambition and his enterprise:

> *The Divine Comedy* expresses everything in the way of emotion, between depravity's despair and the beatific vision, that a man is

capable of experiencing. It is therefore a constant reminder to the poet, of the obligation to explore, to find words for the inarticulate, to capture those feelings which people can hardly even feel, because they have no words for them; and at the same time, a reminder that the explorer beyond the frontiers of ordinary consciousness will only be able to return and report to his fellow citizens, if he has all the time a firm grasp upon the realities with which they are already acquainted.

These two achievements of Dante are not to be thought of as separate or separable. The task of the poet, in making people comprehend the incomprehensible, demands immense resources of language; and in developing the language, enriching the meaning of words and showing how much words can do, he is making possible a much greater range of emotion and perception for other men, because he gives them the speech in which more can be expressed.

For Eliot, "the poetry does not matter" and the poet even less. What matters is what the poetry does, what service it performs for both civilizations and individual readers. Whether or not poetry has any effect whatsoever on culture, either today or in the unimaginable future, it certainly can still perform for people the service Eliot passionately describes. We both say and understand sentences every day that we have never heard before. Most of what can be said has yet to be said. Eliot quite rightly roots that undiscovered territory in human feeling, and the work of poetry, in his view, is to enlarge our capacity for feeling by both using and transcending traditional conventions. This is still the work it must do.

MISTER STEVENS

For Wallace Stevens, poetry was a way of knowing the world. He was interested in it as a subject, and enjoyed it as an activity, but felt its importance as a discipline (like philosophy or history or mathematics) that makes available a kind of knowledge that is otherwise unavailable. If he did not live *in* the work, as Henry James wished to do, he did live through the work, believing poetry is "a sanction of life."

When Stevens uses the word "poetry" in his prose and letters, he usually means it to have this resonance. Writing to Henry Church, a wealthy friend whom he was trying to interest in endowing a Chair for the Study of Poetry, he includes a memorandum:

> What is intended is to study the theory of poetry in relation to what poetry has been and in relation to what it ought to be. Its literature is a part of it, and only a part of it. For this purpose, poetry means not the language of poetry but the thing itself, wherever it may be found. It does not mean verse any more than philosophy means prose.

And he adds, in a later letter to Church, "My belief in poetry is a magnificent fury, or it is nothing"; and, "No one could be more earnest about anything than I am about poetry."

This earnestness about poetry is at the heart of Stevens's best poems, animating them. Its source is less in the subject of the particular poem than in the magnificent fury of his belief in poetry as a way "to live in the world, but outside of existing conceptions of it." As he said in his first public lecture on poetry, "The difficulty of sticking to the true subject, when it is the poetry of the subject that is paramount in one's mind, need only be mentioned to be understood." Of course, especially as Stevens grows older, his recurring subject *is* poetry. His self-consciousness and hermeticism have often been noted, along with the observation that his poems usually touch on the relationship between imagination and reality. But, at least in this century, most poets do not choose their subjects, they are chosen by them, and poetry may have been one of the only subjects Stevens felt much urgency about. If this implies that his poems risk becoming merely expository, it is true that they sometimes succumb to that risk. Consistently, though, when they succeed, the characteristic mode is meditative, not dramatic (as in Frost's poems) or lyric (as in Hart Crane's), even if Stevens would use dramatic and lyric modes within a meditative frame, sometimes switching from one to the other and back again within the course of a single sentence.

There are probably as many ways for a poem to be bad as to be good, but each poet seems to have a habitual way of failing that illuminates his best poems, because that failure makes the worst tendencies in his work show themselves as tendencies his best poems integrate successfully and overcome. For most of his life, Stevens's critical reputation included his early categorization as a dandy, a dilettante, who wrote a kind of "pure poetry" out of affectations of the French tradition. This was Eliot's view of Stevens, until about 1950, and Pound's until the end, and even his own wife is reported to have said in 1915: "I like Mr. Stevens's things when they are not affected, but he writes so much that is affected."

You'd probably have to have a private sanction of life if you were married to someone who thought of your work that way. But, at least in the beginning, Stevens *was* a dandy, consorting with a Greenwich Village crowd his wife despised. For about ten years before they moved to Hartford in 1916, he frequently saw Walter Arensberg and Carl Van Vechten, and less frequently Pitts Sanborn and Mina Loy and Donald Evans (a bohemian aesthete whose poems bear a remarkable resemblance to Stevens's early work), and he even attended a few of the famous salons of Mabel Dodge. Stevens's first publication (excepting in *The Harvard Advocate*) was in Sanborn's magazine, *Trend*, in 1914. As its title implies, *Trend* was trying to be the latest thing and very shocking. Sanborn, who knew Stevens from Harvard, asked him for poems, and Stevens responded with a group made up mostly of pieces from *The Little June Books* that he had written privately for his wife during their courtship five years before, newly arranged with (of course) a French title: "Carnet de Voyage." The publication scandalized his wife and she never forgave him for it.

Stevens's roots were in the Harvard of the nineties: the impressive presence of Santayana, the brilliant ghosts of Moody, Lodge, and Stickney (who had just left for the Sorbonne). Stevens absorbed his French influences independent of Eliot and Pound, and before them—the sensual music of Verlaine rather than the ironies of Laforgue. So after he discarded the then-standard models of Keats and Shelley for an undergraduate's inflated attempts, his poems became a small music:

> And don't you agree with me that if we could get the Michael
> Angeloes out of our heads—Shakespeare, Titian, Goethe—the
> phenomenal men, we should find a multitude of lesser things
> (lesser but a *multitude*) to occupy us? It would be like withdraw-
> ing the sun and bringing out innumerable stars. I do not mean
> the Michael Angeloes are not what they are—but I like Dr. Cam-
> pion, I like Verlaine—water-colors, little statues, small thoughts.
> Let us leave the great things to the professors—.
>
> (Letter to Elsie Moll, December 7, 1908)

Although the book is masterful at concealing it, some of this attitude is still present, undigested and unaltered, in *Harmonium* (published in 1923):

> Ursula, in a garden, found
> A bed of radishes.
> She kneeled upon the ground
> And gathered them,
> With flowers around,
> Blue, gold, pink, and green.

She dreamed in red and gold brocade
And in the grass an offering made
Of radishes and flowers.

A pure sound, a pure "color," a decoration like the rather bad French watercolors he had sent to him by a buyer later in his life, or his exotic imports from China: a poem is merely an object to give pleasure (an attenuated and genteel pleasure).

But this tendency also informs the best poems Stevens ever wrote. I think he probably enjoyed the distance between the poem as an object that "must give pleasure" (a section heading for "Notes Toward a Supreme Fiction") and poetry as a way of knowing the world that provides a sanction of life. There is no question that he believed in each as thoroughly as the other, and that one of the primary satisfactions he took from the act of writing was to bring the two together, to merge and embody them in the poem.

There are two images from Stevens's life which call up these seemingly disparate ideas. The first is the rather well-known one of Stevens composing while walking briskly to work each morning, jotting phrases on tiny scraps of paper in his tiny script, and dropping them on his secretary's desk as he arrived. She would type them during the day, and Stevens, as he left the office, would pick them up. In his younger days, living alone in New York City, he would walk to Connecticut or New Jersey and back, sometimes forty-five miles, on a Sunday. In an article based on an interview in 1941—the only interview Stevens ever granted—he says that he would often walk about with a phrase of Verlaine in his head, "how just one musical French phrase of that poet was exalting enough for the whole day." That physicality—the poem as object, as sound, as sensual music—is as essential to the life of his poems as his belief in the discipline.

However, Stevens's work is not all bright colors and tunk-a-tunk-tunk and "muzzy bellies in parade." There is something else in it—a dark tone of loneliness and isolation—that is called up by another image of Stevens, one which his daughter presented in a lecture at the Huntington Library. She talks about coming upon her father in a dark part of the house sitting in a chair in silence, a habit which mystified and frightened her. On this occasion, she watched him for some time, and finally approached his chair, cautiously touched his knee, and asked what he was doing. "Thinking," he answered gruffly. Later in the lecture, she quotes Stevens's description of his own father from the letters: "'He needed what all of us need, and what most of us don't get: That is to say, discrete affection. . . . The result was that he lived alone,'" and she continues: "In a way that also describes my parents' house and our relationships as I was growing up: we held off from each other—one might say my father lived alone."

The morning and the night, walking briskly and sitting silently, the company of the office and the loneliness of the home: these fusions are part of the richness of Stevens's best poems. But there is a richness, if you will, beneath the richness, an emotional weight that anchors the movement of the mind and the pleasures of the ear, the result both of the magnificent fury of his belief in poetry and the specific character of that belief. "To live in the world but outside of existing conceptions of it" was for Stevens not only an individual life but an isolated one. Of course, such personal isolation finally has little to do with ideas, except in determining them. It is a spiritual condition. His ideas derive from his isolation, not the reverse. Its weight is at the center of Stevens's best work, most obviously in the poems from the end of his life, in *The Rock* and after:

> *You speak. You say:* Today's character is not
> A skeleton out of its cabinet. Nor am I.
>
> The poem about the pineapple, the one
> About the mind as never satisfied,
>
> The one about the credible hero, the one
> About summer, are not what skeletons think about.
>
> I wonder, have I lived a skeleton's life,
> As a disbeliever in reality,
>
> A countryman of all the bones in the world?
> Now, here, the snow I had forgotten becomes

Part of a major reality, part of
An appreciation of a reality

And thus an elevation, as if I left
With something I could touch, touch every way.

And yet nothing has been changed except what is
Unreal, as if nothing had been changed at all.
                              ("As You Leave the Room")

The poem is Stevens's version of "The Circus Animals' Desertion"; at
the end he spoke almost as directly as Yeats, after making a rhetorical
method of ornamentation, avoidance, and concealment. In his letters,
he had addressed his best friend as Mr. Church and referred to his
wife as Mrs. Stevens, and this formality also informed his poetry,
down to the complications of syntax and his amusing, often opaque
titles, which were kept in a separate notebook and usually added last
to the poems.

The time of year has grown indifferent.
Mildew of summer and the deepening snow
Are both alike in the routine I know.
I am too dumbly in my being pent.

The wind attendant on the solstices
Blows on the shutters of the metropoles,
Stirring no poet in his sleep, and tolls
The grand ideas of the villages.

The malady of the quotidian. . . .
Perhaps, if winter once could penetrate
Through all its purples to the final slate,
Persisting bleakly in an icy haze;

One might in turn become less diffident—
Out of such mildew plucking neater mould
And spouting new orations of the cold.
One might. One might. But time will not relent.

Indeed, *one might in turn become less diffident;* but Wallace Stevens would invariably undercut such a personal expression of isolation and malaise with an ironic title such as "The Man Whose Pharynx Was Bad."

Stevens's subject is finally human consciousness, how we see reality and implicitly see ourselves. In a sense, this is the subject of all significant poetry. But Stevens is distinctive because he immersed himself thoroughly in the formal properties of language as if it could make pure music, while holding himself accountable for its inherent reference and meaning, the "necessary angel of the earth." He was able to use poetic form as a means of discovering and extending consciousness. I think this is his importance to poets that have followed him, even if within five years of his death the dominant mode was to write confessional poetry with as little reticence as possible. For any poet who wants to learn, Stevens's work can teach how to use the physicality of the poem to embody abstraction, how to use the ear to see, how potent are the varieties of syntax, and even how to be ambitious in the work instead of in promoting it. That language makes consciousness, rather than the reverse, has recently become a seminal idea in philosophy and the sciences and has remarkable implications. The connection of those disciplines to the discipline of poetry is an idea which would have given Stevens great pleasure.

DISCLOSURES OF POETRY

Wallace Stevens led a fascinating life, but it would not be of interest to the movies. He *did* almost nothing besides walk to the office every day, work, listen to Brahms, scrub the kitchen floor now and then, read a great deal, and write poetry. He made a world through the imagination, but it's a world infused by the actual world: "The imagination loses vitality as it ceases to adhere to what is real" ("The Noble Rider and the Sound of Words"). It's easy to guess how important to him were those early trips to Florida and Cuba and, later, the occasional indulgences he allowed to slip through his Pennsylvania Dutch abnegation, such as the imports from France and China and the limited editions in fine bindings: they were emblems of an extraordinary reality. One of his partners at work said that Stevens would go to any length to get a book he liked specially bound. So it was a significant comment on his private pleasures that, soon after Stevens died, his wife called in the local used-book dealer to haul his library away for the going price of the books themselves, as if they would not have a greater value because they belonged to him. He and his wife apparently had not been on speaking terms for years before his death. When their daughter was born in 1924, Stevens moved to the attic to be out of the way. His early journals, found after his wife's death, had been edited with a pair of scissors; exactly what was excised or why or by whom is not known. What remained of these journals makes up his daughter Holly's *Souvenirs and Prophecies,* a necessarily sketchy biography-in-documents of Stevens's early years. Holly

Stevens herself has been forthcoming about the embittered atmosphere of the household, the withdrawal of her father and mother from each other, into mutual isolation. As A. Walton Litz says in *Introspective Voyager: The Poetic Development of Wallace Stevens*, "The experience at the center of *Ideas of Order* is one of deprivation, a sense and acceptance of 'nothing that is not there and the nothing that is.'" The great deprivation of Stevens's life was that of human intimacy. He was apparently incapable of it. He wrote about it, obliquely, again and again. "Farewell to Florida" was written between the two editions of *Ideas of Order* (the Alcestis Press edition in 1935 and the Knopf trade edition a year later); when Stevens added the poem to the Knopf edition, he placed it at the front of the volume, as the program piece. It can and should be read as a poem about the direction of his imagination, from the lush South to the stark North, but the poem is also about the end of love. This is its first stanza:

> Go on, high ship, since now, upon the shore,
> The snake has left its skin upon the floor.
> Key West sank downward under massive clouds
> And silvers and greens spread over the sea. The moon
> Is at the mast-head and the past is dead.
> Her mind will never speak to me again.
> I am free. High above the mast the moon
> Rides clear of her mind and the waves make a refrain
> Of this: that the snake has shed its skin upon
> The floor. Go on through the darkness. The waves fly back.

This way of reading the poem would have certainly displeased Stevens. He said, at about the time he wrote it, "There is nothing that kills an idea like expressing it in personal terms." Always there is this pull in his work toward the cold purity of abstraction, the "mind of winter." This indicates both his poetry's strength and its limits. It works best when it also contains the opposite pull of the concrete and personal. Like Yeats, Stevens constantly strives toward objectivity in his poems, but where Yeats explicitly embodies his personal passion, his lust and rage, and makes them part of the poetic drama, Stevens's characteristic strategy is to stay off-stage, behind the curtain. Yet Stevens's poetic instrument was so fine and subtle, and his range so various, that he could even (indirectly) address what was missing:

Re-statement of Romance

The night knows nothing of the chants of night.
It is what it is as I am what I am:
And in perceiving this I best perceive myself

And you. Only we two may interchange
Each in the other what each has to give.
Only we two are one, not you and night,

Not night and I, but you and I, alone,
So much alone, so deeply by ourselves,
So far beyond the casual solitudes,

That night is only the background of our selves,
Supremely true each to its separate self,
In the pale light that each upon the other throws.

Stevens's best poems are thoroughly informed by the sense that writing for him was his greatest pleasure and that part of this pleasure was to be as serious and ambitious in them as possible. He wrote poems, as well as everything else he wrote, because he wanted to. He could take any risk in his poetry because his livelihood did not depend on it. The humor, the zaniness, the exuberance, the wry amusement at human quirkiness that pervades his letters is also a quality of his poetry—along with the restraint, formality, and reserve that sometimes make him seem ungiving and ungenerous. "Thy rose-lipped arch-archangelic jeune"—the way he signed a letter to his mother at age sixteen—lived constantly inside a man who appears to have been old all his life.

So Stevens's poems, and his temperament, can be seen most accurately as occurring within a play of contraries or a tension of oppositions: high talk and plain diction, gay and somber tones, invention and discovery, imagination and reality, the theory of poetry and its practice, the one charcoal gray suit he had remade every few years from the same pattern and the same bolt of cloth and the multicolored ties he occasionally wore and referred to as "a bit of Florida." If his poems wear clothes, some dress as he did in identical somber suits with only a touch of color at the neck, but others are decked out in wild Florida outfits with a charcoal gray tie. There is no example from his poems that stands as a pure instance of one or the other term of opposition. This is the point: it is the tension itself that is generative, however it may be generated. According to Coleridge, who greatly influenced Stevens's thinking about poetry, the imagination of the poet reveals itself in "the balance or reconcilement of opposite or discordant qualities." The poems in *Harmonium* can be described as tending toward one pole or the other, but never resting there. "Two Figures in Dense Violet Light" is a highly personal poem about sexual intimacy made "objective" by its title (the same strategy he uses for "The Man Whose Pharynx Was Bad"). It's characterized by plain diction and poignant statement, but there is also a wild opening that is very funny ("I had as lief be embraced by the porter at the hotel / As to get no more from the moonlight / Than your moist hand"), not to mention the "puerile" and those "buzzards . . . on the ridge-pole" in the penultimate stanza. At the opposite extreme is "The Emperor of Ice Cream," whose diction is so gay and gaudy in describing the simple, somber situation of a woman's death. But near the end of the poem Stevens slips in one dark, bitter, direct line in the plain style— "they come / to show how cold she is, and dumb"—and it is this line that determines the poem's final tone amidst what Stevens called its "essential gaudiness," which, he said on a later occasion, made him choose it as his favorite among his poems.

When I went through Stevens's papers and what's left of his personal library at the Huntington Library in California, I found two entries in a notebook of single lines that seem to me to represent the opposite extremes in his poetry. As far as I know, he never used either of them in a poem. The entries are "gasping magnitudes" and "a child playing with a ball." The first seems generated wholly out of language, the two short *a* sounds: a pure invention in language which then becomes a fact in the world. The second entry ("a child playing with a ball") is, by contrast, in an almost transparent style, referring without attention to itself to a simple dramatic scene in the world. At issue underlying these extremes of diction is an important philosophical question: how do you get *through* language to what Stevens calls "the veritable *ding-an-sich* at last," to the thing-in-itself? In other words: how do you *know?*

The question as it comes to play in Stevens's poems has profound implications. As soon as one says this, however, the *poetry* must be remembered and its primacy asserted, even if some of his later poems read like wintry philosophy of mind. In 1941, responding to a Yale undergraduate who had asked for help in explicating one of his poems, Stevens wrote:

> As a matter of fact, from my point of view, the quality called poetry is quite as precious as meaning. The truth is that, since I am far more interested in poetry than I am in philosophy, it is even more precious. But it would take a lot of letter writing to get anywhere with this.

Stevens, in fact, did a lot of letter writing. His daughter's edition of his letters is 890 pages and 992 letters long and is only a selection of the more than 3,300 that were available. It's an invaluable resource in understanding his poetry and his ideas as well as his temperament, and as such still represents the best critical biography that we have. In saying "the quality called poetry" is even more precious than meaning, Stevens is trying to point to the essential quality of the poem itself, the poem-as-poem. If he never explains in his letters or essays precisely what he means by "the quality called poetry," it's because for him that quality can only be found in the poem itself, in its particular words in their particular arrangement. This is what he calls "disclosures of poetry":

> The function of the poet at any time is to discover by his own thought and feeling what seems to him to be poetry at that time. Ordinarily he will disclose what he finds in his own poetry by way of the poetry itself. He exercises this function most often without being conscious of it, so that the disclosures in his poetry, while they define what seems to him to be poetry, are disclosures of poetry, not disclosures of definitions of poetry. ("Introduction," *The Necessary Angel*)

The poet writes what seems to him to be poetry—the tautology would be useless except for Stevens's emphasis on *poetry* in contradistinction to its meaning, which is merely one aspect of poetry but the one that dominates the response of most readers. This response was especially prevalent in the mid-thirties, when the atmosphere of worldwide upheaval and the latter days of the Depression provoked among intellectuals a general questioning of any writing without social purpose or political content. Stevens wrote a number of poems in ironic, aggressive reaction to that atmosphere, including "Mr. Burnshaw and the Statue," but even of that poem he said in 1935: "My principal concern with this poem (and, I suppose, with any poem) is not so much with the ideas as with the poetry of the thing." In other contexts, he strikes this emphasis even harder, asserting that "[s]ubject is merely the opportunity for poetry," and, in *Adagia* (a collection of his epigrams and aphorisms he stored in a notebook), "[t]here is no wing like meaning." Finally, in 1937, he writes in "The Man with the Blue Guitar," parodying Flaubert's line about Madame Bovary and deflecting it: "Tom-tom, *c'est moi*. The blue guitar / And I are one."

At this point in Stevens's life, what matters most about an idea or a subject or a "meaning" is what can be made out of it, and what can be made out of it is, in Stevens's view, a result of the poet's personality. This is "the irrational element in poetry," which is also the title of a lecture Stevens interspersed with a reading of his own poems at Harvard in 1936 (reprinted as an essay in *Opus Posthumous*):

A day or two before Thanksgiving we had a light fall of snow in Hartford. It melted a little by day and then froze again at night, forming a thin, bright crust over the grass. At the same time, the moon was almost full. I awoke once several hours before daylight and as I lay in bed I heard the steps of a cat running over the snow under my window almost inaudibly. The faintness and strangeness of the sound made on me one of those impressions one so often seizes as pretexts for poetry.

I want to look at "The Idea of Order at Key West" in terms of its sound and its syntax, because I take sound and syntax to be the primary aspects, with structure and content, of *poetry* as Stevens uses the word. Two biographical facts dominate the background of its composition. First, Stevens was promoted to vice-president of the Hartford Accident and Indemnity Company in 1934. His work at the office was very important to him—so much so, that when it came time to retire he refused, and eventually refused the Charles Eliot Norton Chair in Poetry at Harvard at the age of seventy-four because he was afraid if he took a year's leave of absence the company would not allow him to return to his job. The second fact seems clearly related to the first: he began writing prolifically in 1934 after a virtual silence of nearly ten years, beginning a period of extraordinary productivity that would last until he died. After writing one book of poems in his first fifty-four years, he wrote five books from 1934 to 1942, including two long poems on the subject of the imagination, "The Man with the Blue Guitar" and "Notes Toward a Supreme Fiction." His promotion seemed to free him to write. The worldly success and material comfort that meant so much to him were sufficiently assured, and he gave himself wholeheartedly to a life of the mind through poetry until he died in 1954. It's no wonder that so many of these poems are about poetry and the imagination: this was what he did and how he lived.

"The Idea of Order at Key West," though unique in the volume in which it first appeared, should be seen as the program piece for this twenty years' volume of work. It's his first serious foray into an explicit straightforward rendering of the Romantic poem of the Imagination—without the irony and self-mockery that permeates "The Comedian as the Letter C." It was initially published in October 1934 as one of a group of eight poems appearing in the first issue of an elegant little magazine called *Alcestis* (Stevens's first significant publication since *Harmonium* eleven years earlier). The magazine was edited by Ronald Lane Latimer, who published the first edition of *Ideas of Order* under the Alcestis imprint in 1935 and also conducted an interesting correspondence with Stevens about his life and work during the mid-thirties. Writing to Latimer on November 15, 1935, Stevens glosses some of the ideas in "The Idea of Order at Key West," and, as is his habit in these years, he concludes his remarks with an assertion of his primary interest in the poetry of the thing:

In "The Idea of Order at Key West" life has ceased to be a matter of chance. It may be that every man introduces his own order into the life about him and that the idea of order in general is simply what Bishop Berkeley might have called a fortuitous concourse of personal orders. But still there is order. This is the sort of development you are looking for. But, then, I never thought it was a fixed philosophic proposition that life was a mass of irrelevancies any more than I now think it is a fixed proposition that every man introduces his own order as part of a general order. These are tentative ideas for the purposes of poetry.

The ideas of the poem operate as part of its texture, no more important, and no less, than its syntax, its structure, and its sonority. Stevens would have us feel these as equal claims on our attention in reading the poem. We are not accustomed to hearing or using language this way, although this is the way language is used in poetry, especially in modern poetry and particularly in Stevens's poetry. Its discursive "meaning" is a part of its texture but only a part. The idea was not unique to Stevens. Hart Crane—who in the early twenties wrote that Stevens's work "makes the rest of us look like quail"—said every poem is "a new word." If you read "The Idea of Order at Key West" aloud and listen for the variety of the sentences and their relationship to one another against the pattern of a gorgeously strict blank verse punctuated by a few strategic end-rhymes, you can feel these formal elements of the verse orchestrating the meaning and ideas of the poem.

> She sang beyond the genius of the sea.
> The water never formed to mind or voice,
> Like a body wholly body, fluttering
> Its empty sleeves; and yet its mimic motion
> Made constant cry, caused constantly a cry,
> That was not ours although we understood,
> Inhuman, of the veritable ocean.
>
> The sea was not a mask. No more was she.
> The song and water were not medleyed sound

Even if what she sang was what she heard,
Since what she sang was uttered word by word.
It may be that in all her phrases stirred
The grinding water and the gasping wind;
But it was she and not the sea we heard.

For she was the maker of the song she sang.
The ever-hooded, tragic-gestured sea
Was merely a place by which she walked to sing.
Whose spirit is this? we said, because we knew
It was the spirit that we sought and knew
That we should ask this often as she sang.

If it was only the dark voice of the sea
That rose, or even colored by many waves;
If it was only the outer voice of sky
And cloud, of the sunken coral water-walled,
However clear, it would have been deep air,
The heaving speech of air, a summer sound
Repeated in a summer without end
And sound alone. But it was more than that,
More even than her voice, and ours, among
The meaningless plungings of water and the wind,
Theatrical distances, bronze shadows heaped
On high horizons, mountainous atmospheres
Of sky and sea.
                    It was her voice that made
The sky acutest at its vanishing.
She measured to the hour its solitude.
She was the single artificer of the world
In which she sang. And when she sang, the sea,
Whatever self it had, became the self
That was her song, for she was the maker. Then we,
As we beheld her striding there alone,
Knew that there never was a world for her
Except the one she sang and, singing, made.

Ramon Fernandez, tell me, if you know,
Why, when the singing ended and we turned
Toward the town, tell why the glassy lights,
The lights in the fishing boats at anchor there,
As the night descended, tilting in the air,
Mastered the night and portioned out the sea,
Fixing emblazoned zones and fiery poles,
Arranging, deepening, enchanting night.

Oh! Blessed rage for order, pale Ramon,
The maker's rage to order words of the sea,
Words of the fragrant portals, dimly-starred,
And of ourselves and of our origins,
In ghostlier demarcations, keener sounds.

Stevens said later, "Ramon Fernandez was not intended to be anyone at all. I chose two everyday Spanish names. I knew of Ramon
Fernandez, the critic, and had read some of his criticisms but I did
not have him in mind." Stevens could have read a few of Fernandez's
essays in *The Dial,* the best and best-known literary journal of the
twenties, and in the Paris weeklies he had delivered to Hartford, but
Fernandez's criticism bears no substantial relationship to the poem.
Stevens's choice of the name for the pure sound and flavor of it, however, reveals one aspect of his poetic method. "Ramon Fernandez, tell
me, if you know" is an unusually euphonious line; if you can't hear it,
substitute the name of another critic: "Samuel Coleridge, tell me, if
you know." It maintains the meter, except to replace the initial iamb
with a trochee (*Sam* u instead of Ra *mon*), the most common metrical
substitution in blank verse. But what's lost are the internal *n* sounds
that punctuate the line and lead into the initial *n* sound of the last
word: "Ramo*n* Fer*n*andez, tell me, if you k*n*ow." Those *n*s cause us to
stress the word "know" even harder than its metrical and rhetorical
stress requires, and it is a crucial word to the meaning of the poem,
but, more importantly for Stevens's purposes, the interweaving of the
sound contributes to the solidity of the verse, to bring the language
itself to our attention, not only what it signifies. The duration of the

syllables of the two names is also quite different, and, although there is no way to systematize quantitative metrics in English (since its syllables do not have a measurably consistent time value as they do in classical Greek and Latin, whose prosodic terminology we borrow), the syllables of "Ramon Fernandez" are apprehensibly longer, and make a music of this line which the five separate vowel sounds of "Sam-u-el Cole-ridge" would not. Stevens points to the role of the ear in writing poems in "The Irrational Element in Poetry":

> You can compose poetry in whatever form you like. If it seems a seventeenth-century habit to begin lines with capital letters, you can go in for liquid transitions of greater simplicity; and so on. It is not that nobody cares. It matters immensely. The slightest sound matters. The most momentary rhythm matters. You can do as you please, yet everything matters. . . . You have somehow to know the sound that is the exact sound; and you do in fact know, without knowing how. Your knowledge is irrational.

Everything matters; yet *how* does it matter? Stevens never says exactly in his prose, because he believes that it is not possible to say except by its embodiment in a poem, the only actual and accurate disclosure of poetry. In a later essay, "Effects of Analogy," he calls the music of poetry "a mode of analogy" and "a communication of emotion" and leaves it there. Although the music of poetry is quite different from music, their effects are similar and the problems of description the same. No one would call Stevens's beloved Brahms's Violin Concerto inane, and yet how do you describe it in such a way as to articulate its meaning, much less to approximate the experience of listening to it? As Suzanne Langer says in *Philosophy in a New Key*, its meaning is nondiscursive, not paraphrasable, nonlinear, or, as Stevens says, "irrational." The same is true of the music of poetry, though a complication arises because this music is comprised of sounds that are potentially meaningful in a discursive way, and this "distraction" is why many readers have difficulty hearing the music. In fact, reversing the usual terms of comparison provides the clearest analogy. Poetry is not as much a kind of music as music is a kind of writing. Both poetry and music are writing. Their forms, like all temporal art forms, are shaped by sequence and pattern.

Look at the first stanza of "The Idea of Order at Key West":

She sang beyond the genius of the sea.
The water never formed to mind or voice,
Like a body wholly body, fluttering
Its empty sleeves; and yet its mimic motion
Made constant cry, caused constantly a cry,
That was not ours although we understood,
Inhuman, of the veritable ocean.

The absolute regularity of the iambic beat in the first two lines, varied by the trochaic third line; the orchestration of the long *e* sound in line one; the excessive alliteration in "its mimic motion / Made constant cry, caused constantly a cry" relieved by the variety of vowels with no alliteration or even any hard consonants in the next line ("That was not ours although we understood"): these have physiological effects on our nervous system, as do all the formal properties of the language which are more difficult to notice and less possible to describe. The sound of the poem, the cadence of the language, keeps us physically engaged with words that are always threatening to disappear into meaning. The poem is packed with sound-linkage and repetition; you can plot it by isolating the sounds of each syllable and following their repetition and modulation in relationship to the rhythm, the stresses and pauses, of the blank verse.

But the achievement of "The Idea of Order at Key West" is best revealed by its syntax. There is an important way in which syntax (the arrangement of the words in sentences, and the inter-relationship of the sentences) is an aspect of the sound of the poem. None of the categories we use to describe the poem's work—rhythm, sound, syntax, structure, content—are absolutely discrete in the poem itself, where everything is going on at once. It's because so many things are going on at once that poems can affect us so thoroughly. We want that richness. Anything less complex feels mechanical, predetermined, thought-out. But the syntax of a poem also gives its reader a self-contained experience of movement that in the case of "The Idea of

Order at Key West" is memorable in the same way that the experience of movement in Brahms's Violin Concerto is memorable after hearing it a certain number of times. As each occurs in time, sequentially, it enacts its overall pattern. In poetry this is primarily the function of syntax; syntax is both the logic and the dance. No one is better at it than Stevens. It seems to me the main generative force of his later poems. You can feel them being made through the agency of the sentences, the possible turns and complications and pleasures of syntax. The syntax forms the skeleton on which the substance of the poem grows as it grows, and like the skeleton, the syntax determines the shape of the flesh attached to it, hence the body's beauty or ugliness. At the same time, the syntax makes a pure arrangement apart from any other aspect of the poem related to it (rhythm, sound, structure, content), a pattern of movement like music.

Stevens's use of syntax in "The Idea of Order at Key West" reflects the play of contraries and tension between extremes that characterizes his poetic method in general—in this case, between the extremes of the two poetic traditions that influenced him. At one pole is the tradition of English poetry until the end of the nineteenth century, a poetry in which syntax is primarily a grammatical articulation of the poem's substance—its argument, ideas, and drama—a syntax whose first purpose is to organize content. At the opposite pole is the tradition of French poetry from the nineteenth to early-twentieth century, deriving first from the *symbolistes* and then, particularly with regard to syntax, from the poems and theories of Mallarmé and Valéry. Stevens held a lifelong interest in this poetry and aesthetics. One of the last projects of his life was to write introductions to two of Valéry's aesthetic dialogues, published in the Bollingen series in 1955. Valéry was responsible for defining "pure poetry," the crucial ingredient of which is syntax as pure arrangement, as an expressive structure in and of itself. In 1935, in response to Latimer's ongoing interrogation about his work and his influences, Stevens begins a disclaimer of Valéry and a dismissal of the question of influence in general and ends up confirming Valéry's influence in the way in which that word makes the most sense: "an effect derived from the mass of things I have read in the past." Here is the passage:

I have read very little of Valéry, although I have a number of his books and, for that matter, several books about him. If there are any literary relations between my things and those of other writers, they are unconscious. Such a thing as adopting the method or the manner of another writer is inconceivable. Granted the strong effect of literature, it is an effect derived from the mass of things I have read in the past. Of course, a man like Valéry emerges from his books without close reading.

The thrust of French symbolism was, for reasons political as well as literary, "to wring the neck of rhetoric," to destroy the syntax of prose discourse and therefore its logic while, in Mallarmé's phrase, "yield[ing] the initiative to the words." Valéry, speaking of Mallarmé's syntax, defined pure poetry in these terms:

> In this [that is, Mallarmé's interest in syntax] he approached the attitude of men who in algebra have examined the science of forms and the symbolical part of the art of mathematics. This type of attention makes the structure of expressions more felt and more interesting than their significance or value. Properties of transformations of attention are worthier the mind's attention than what they transform.

It was exactly on this basis that *Harmonium* and *Ideas of Order* were attacked by many early critics. John Crowe Ransom (in *The World's Body*) said it was "poetry for poetry's sake, and you cannot get a moral out of it." Stevens provoked some of this by calling *Ideas of Order* a volume of "pure poetry" in his preface to the Knopf edition. The term is terrifically misleading applied to Stevens's poetry, but I think it does articulate one of the extremes of his interest in syntax. As Donald Davie says in *Articulate Energy*, "The syntax of Mallarmé appeals to nothing but itself, to nothing outside the world of the poem." This is certainly not the case in any of Stevens's poems, but they are formed from the tension between syntax as an articulation of content and as an expressive structure in itself.

There is only one violation of normal word order in "The Idea of Order at Key West": the placement of the relative clause between the noun and adjective at the end of the first stanza ("and yet its mimic motion/Made constant cry, caused constantly a cry, / *That was not ours although we understood,* / Inhuman, of the veritable ocean"). I've talked about one way the clause operates sonically, as relief from the preceding alliteration; and the rearrangement of usual syntax could also be justified by the content, as emphasis. The sentence is impossible to reorder without disfiguring it entirely. There is one predicate-less "sentence" in the poem (the final stanza) which, again in terms of content, is a kind of summing up by exclamatory naming and thereby contains an action. But I want to call attention to the sentences in themselves, apart from their content: their individuality and the proportions of their relationship. It is this relationship that Stevens wants to count, embodying, as Coleridge said, the "variety in unity, and unity in variety" which characterizes art and which may also be a quality we wish for in our lives. If so, the relationship of the sentences might be said to be mimetic in the deepest sense, but in any case the overall syntax is a source of interest and engagement as a pattern unfolding in time, at the same time that it presents the content of the poem. Poets as different as Stevens, Williams, Pound, Eliot, and Crane all felt a debt to the *symbolistes* for bringing to their attention the possibility of using syntax as music or mathematics. The *symbolistes'* influence on Eliot and Pound was quite direct, appearing as the dislocation of syntax in *The Waste Land* and *The Cantos* and, less directly, in Williams's *Spring and All,* all of Hart Crane's poems, and most of the best-known poetry of the twenties (with the notable exceptions of Frost and Hardy, who continued to work in the English tradition). More than any other single quality, the violation of syntax for expressive purposes characterizes the poetry that has since come to be known as "modernist." It continues to be common among contemporary poets (like John Ashbery, Jorie Graham, and Charles Wright) who otherwise have little in common and none of the political agenda that originally engendered it.

In "The Idea of Order at Key West," this syntax-as-arrangement can be detected primarily in the pattern of the whole rather than in the construction of the individual sentences. However, I do want to isolate two remarkable sentences from the poem, both of which vividly incorporate both of Stevens's syntactical impulses. The first sentence begins the fourth stanza:

> If it was only the dark voice of the sea
> That rose, or even colored by many waves;
> If it was only the outer voice of sky
> And cloud, of the sunken coral water-walled,
> However clear, it would have been deep air,
> The heaving speech of air, a summer sound
> Repeated in a summer without end
> And sound alone.

There is a clear propositional logic in the sentence, two conditions and a conclusion: if it was x, if it was y, it would have been z. I take that to be the bare skeleton of the sentence. While the embellishment is obviously what makes the sentence, the solidity of the skeleton underneath allows, even promotes, the embellishment. In combination, they make the sentence interesting as a sentence. The first two pairs of lines have a parallel phrasing that almost obscures the grammatical difference between the relative clause ("The sea / That rose, or even colored by many waves") and the prepositional phrases ("Of sky / And cloud, of the sunken coral water-walled"); the latter constitute the first of the syntactical repetitions, the embellishments, by which the rest of the sentence is generated: the appositional phrases ("it would have been deep air, / The heaving speech of air, a summer sound") that lead into the final clause. This syntax orchestrates the repetition of the nouns (air, summer, sound) in a kind of dance of these central elements of the poem. This way of making a sentence, so crucial to Stevens's work, can be directly traced to Mallarmé and Valéry and Stevens's attachment to French poetry.

The same dual attitude toward syntax (as logical articulation and as pure arrangement) is also evident in the remarkable sentence that is the penultimate stanza of the poem. You can hear the arrangement, the movement, through the repetitions of "tell," "why," "lights," and "night." But there is also propositional sense gained by suspending the predicates "mastered" and "portioned" from their subject "the glassy lights" at the end of line three: the lights, the night, and the sea—elements of the dramatic scene in the intervening lines—are yoked by the predications into a relationship with one another that implies a way of seeing not just the harbor in Key West but the world at large. And once again the sentence finds a way to extend itself, this time by means of the participles in the last two lines:

> Ramon Fernandez, tell me, if you know,
> Why, when the singing ended and we turned
> Toward the town, tell why the glassy lights,
> The lights in the fishing boats at anchor there,
> As the night descended, tilting in the air,
> Mastered the night and portioned out the sea,
> Fixing emblazoned zones and fiery poles,
> Arranging, deepening, enchanting night.

What a powerful verb "mastered" becomes through its syntactical placement, and the trochaic substitution at the head of the line drives it rhythmically through its predication—a prosodic device straight out of the tradition of English blank verse to tighten the sinew of the verse.

Even the title, "The Idea of Order at Key West," indicates Stevens's characteristic habit of mind, the play of contraries, setting the metaphysical thrust of the abstraction against the particularity of the place. And, also characteristically, in his playfulness Stevens is most serious, deflecting both his personal isolation and his personal investment in writing onto the unnamed female singer ("there never was a world for her / Except the one she sang and, singing, made"). As for the title, as he said in "The Irrational Element in Poetry," "one writes poetry out of a delight in the harmonious and orderly." In response to a *Partisan Review* questionnaire in 1948, Stevens reworded his earlier statement to the Yale undergraduate:

> Poetic order is potentially as significant as philosophic order. . . .
> There probably is available in reality something accessible through
> a theory of poetry which would make a profound difference in
> our sense of the world.

This is the subject of "The Idea of Order at Key West," a subject that would occupy Stevens for his last twenty years, a subject complicated and enriched by the form of verse, the flexibility of the English sentence, and the poem's structure. "The Idea of Order at Key West" sets up like "Sunday Morning," insofar as there is a third-person narration of an unidentified female character. But whereas "Sunday Morning" maintains that strategy throughout, the narrator quoting and commenting on the character, and being omniscient enough to know such things as "Death is the mother of beauty," the speaker of "The Idea of Order at Key West" identifies himself in the sixth line of the poem as human and part of a group, which turns out to be group of two: him (or her) and Ramon Fernandez. This narrative strategy provides an interesting perspective on the subject of the poem, a perspective capable of shifts and changes that can be traced through the pronouns, and allows Stevens the distance to disclose the depths and dimensions of his own personal engagement with poetry, emotionally and intellectually, as theory and as practice. As such, "The Idea of Order at Key West" may be his fullest disclosure of poetry. It's certainly one of his most beautiful.

A DARK GRAY FLAME

Elizabeth Bishop's poetry is rarely portentous or grand, and never pretentious or grandiose. It may be that her honoring traditional decorum—in both the social and literary meanings of the word—provided her with the sanction to speak plainly and otherwise unceremoniously within proscribed limits. In an essay entitled "Feeling and Precision," Marianne Moore said, "we must be as clear as our natural reticence allows us to be"—a statement Bishop surely completely agreed with. Reticence, which is first a character trait of the poet, is made to serve a formal function in the poetry. It becomes the guiding principle of technique. It pervades the tone and, transliterated into decorum, even defines the range of style and subject within which technique can be employed.

This may explain why, despite many significant differences, Bishop's poetry at its worst and Moore's poetry at its worst both deflate to polite prose that is "too detailedly and objectively descriptive." This was the single qualification of Randall Jarrell's lifelong admiration for Bishop's poetry, and characterizes for me its occasional failure and constant risk, a risk that could not be more unlike that of the poetry of her dominant male contemporaries—Lowell, Berryman, Schwartz, Roethke, and Jarrell himself—whose common ambition was to exceed limits (and also, it seems, one another), decorum having been left very early by the wayside. Part of Bishop's characteristic risk also results from what the New Critics used to call "strategy": observed daily life is lucidly presented by a civilized, intelligent speaker. (One can almost hear Berryman or Schwartz asking, Where is the poetry in *that?*) So when she makes something arresting out of something ordinary—a big fish in a little rented boat, a dentist's waiting room, the sea at the fishhouses—the transformation is remarkably powerful because it seems to occur immediately and necessarily through an act of perception, not as an act of the poet's will. We never feel pushed by rhetoric. And the tone, of course, is essential to this effect.

One of Bishop's favorite poets was George Herbert because of what she called his "absolute naturalness of tone," and from the beginning she aspired to this in her own poetry, in conjunction with the associated virtues of decorum—accuracy, modesty, restraint, elegance, wit, and impeccable craft—that brought on her the reputation of a "poet's poet." But Herbert has a charged subject that makes his "absolute naturalness of tone" dramatic; Bishop does not wrestle with the weakness of the flesh nor agonize over her salvation. Her agony—when it *is* a felt presence—is always withheld, never explained, and certainly never indulged and, as a result, sometimes acquires the power of a kept secret, although such reticence, less skillfully handled, can seem merely coy. Again the effect depends largely on tone, which, when it comes to personal emotions, may in turn depend on how the poet takes herself in public and to what extent she thinks writing is a public act. The fierce protection of personal privacy has often been the motive behind the strict adherence to a code of social manners; for all her isolation and exile, Bishop wrote from the beginning with a sharp awareness that she was being read.

Late in her life, she sometimes characterized her poems as "just description" and—as Richard Wilbur said in his memorial tribute to her—"lamented her want of a comprehensive philosophy." These remarks have been dismissed by her admirers, but Bishop herself knew very well that the religious passion of Herbert and Hopkins (another of her favorites) was the fuel for their poetry, and no doubt knew what their poetry paradoxically gained by being subordinate to belief and only one manifestation of their service to God. "A Cold Spring," with its epigraph from Hopkins, is in fact not much more than "just description" partially because it has no fervor, religious or otherwise.

The epigraph not only asks us to read the poem as a commentary on Hopkins's "Spring," which may make her poem more interesting, but also invites us to compare the two poems and, by comparison, Bishop's secular Spring, with its tepid affection, is very cold indeed.

Significantly, the most excited and acute line in "A Cold Spring" is a description—in this case, of fireflies rising from the grass at dusk: "—exactly like the bubbles in champagne." The punctuation and adverb call extra attention to a moment when language transparently renders the world because of the mind's ability to perceive similarity amid dissimilarity. For both Aristotle and Coleridge, this is the root of metaphor and the basis of poetic genius. It is also, I think, at the source of Elizabeth Bishop's passion. Like the sandpiper in her poem, she was "a student of Blake," attempting, in Blake's terms, "to cleanse the doors of perception" as consistently in her work as Hopkins celebrated God in his. At their best, her descriptions take on the life not only of what's described but also of the describer, and effectively enact and embody her special being-in-the-world partially because there is no "comprehensive philosophy" to interfere with the vision or the rendering (although there is certainly, as Henry James would say, a "central intelligence": hers). The character speaking and sometimes explicitly writing her poems is characterized by what she says, what she sees, and what she says about what she sees, and this character is unusually consistent in her work. Her curiosity is lively. She looks very hard and very gently at things. A good part of our response to an Elizabeth Bishop poem is to *her*. Her genius was the degree to which she found the technique to get herself, with her own peculiar temperament and predilections, into her poetry and onto the page.

North & South, published when she was thirty-five, is one of those rare first volumes in which a poet appears already fully developed and accomplished, but she had been "a student of Blake" for a long time before that. Like Keats's negative capability, apparent in his letters before he discovered the technique to make use of it in his poems, Bishop's talent for intense observation entered her prose before she could get it into her poetry. The following passage is from a prose sketch published when she was only twenty-two, in the May 1933 issue of the *Vassar Journal of Undergraduate Studies:*

As I waited I heard a multitude of small sounds, and knew simultaneously that I had been hearing them all along—sounds high in the air, of a faintly rhythmic regularity, yet resembling the retreat of innumerable small waves, lake-waves, rustling on sand.

Of course it was the birds going South. They were very high up, a fairly large sort of bird, I couldn't tell what, but almost speck-like, paying no attention to even the highest trees or steeples. They spread across a wide swath of sky, each rather alone, and at first their wings seemed all to be beating perfectly together. But by watching one bird, then another, I saw that some flew a little slower than others, some were trying to get ahead and some flew at an individual rubato; each seemed a variation, and yet altogether my eyes were deceived into thinking them perfectly precise and regular. I watched closely the spaces between the birds. It was as if there were an invisible thread joining all the outside birds and within this fragile network they possessed the sky.

Those familiar with Eastern meditation techniques will recognize in this passage exercises to alter the brain's habits of perception, but "watching the spaces between" is also a way to learn how to see that can be found in any number of treatises on painting and drawing. Bishop told an interviewer in 1966:

I think I'm more visual than most poets. . . . All my life I've been interested in painting. . . . As a child I was dragged round the Boston Museum of Fine Arts and Mrs. Gardner's museum and the Fogg.

In an essay published the same year, Howard Moss praised Bishop's "unique exactitude of detail" in these terms:

Nothing that has not been isolated to be examined, nothing that has not been delineated sharply has been permitted to be written down. These poems are so pure we feel their author has been fed on a secret literature unknown to the rest of the world. Has she read the histories of stones, mountains and waterfalls in their original languages?

The answer seems to have been yes. Although we may think of it as passive, observation for Bishop was an activity, even a passionate activity: *ob* + *servare* 'toward,' 'for' + 'to keep,' 'to hold.' If her violent early losses of her father and mother are borne in mind, the Latin root of "observe" may reveal the root of her passion for and in observation: *toward keeping, for holding.* Her life-as-observer surely fed her writing and vice versa, in locales from Nova Scotia to Brazil, even when what she looked at was the magic-lantern show of her own memories.

This begins to locate for me the essential strangeness of her work. From "The Fish":

I looked into his eyes
which were far larger than mine
but shallower, and yellowed,
the irises backed and packed
with tarnished tinfoil
seen through the lenses
of old scratched isinglass.
They shifted a little, but not
to return my stare.
—It was more like the tipping
of an object toward the light.
I admired his sullen face,
the mechanism of his jaw,
and then I saw
that from his lower lip
—if you could call it a lip—
grim, wet, and weaponlike,
hung five old pieces of fish-line,
or four and a wire leader
with the swivel still attached,
with all their five big hooks
grown firmly in his mouth.

If love desires intimate knowledge, and therefore shows itself in close observation, Bishop's fish is lovingly rendered without a milligram of sentimentality. Almost nothing happens in the poem. She had already caught the "tremendous fish" as the poem begins, and all she does is look at it (including its *eyes*) and release it. But the observation itself is dramatic, frequently corrected and qualified as in so many of her poems, and dramatizes not exactly self-effacement but self-definition as "a believer in total immersion" (a phrase from "At the Fish-houses"): in a passionate, disinterested, total attention that here produces an ecstatic if not unambiguously joyful release from the self ("I stared and stared . . . until everything / was rainbow, rainbow, rainbow!").

In this sense, "The Fish" can be read as a meditative poem that has nothing whatsoever to do with St. Ignatius's Jesuit meditation formula of memory, understanding, and will, or the English metaphysical poetry influenced by it. There's no thinking aloud, no muscular logic or forged conceits. The mind of the speaker only becomes apparent when it shows the distinction between itself and what it sees, through its qualifications ("—It was more like the tipping / of an object toward the light"; "—if you could call it a lip—"; "five old pieces of fishline, / or four and a wire leader"). But the mind is embodied everywhere she looks, and its releasing and attaching itself to the object is all the more engaging because the object is so grotesque—a diseased, lice-infested fish, whose "brown skin hung in strips / like ancient wallpaper"—an image of life suffered, battered, exhausted, nearly finished. Yet the fish is still alive. The last line of the poem ("And I let the fish go") could hardly be more simple in itself or more resonant in its context, an accumulated richness finding the plainest possible diction.

Formally, the complex and subtle effects of such moments in Bishop's poetry fall under the sturdy rubric of pattern-and-variation, not only in the meter—where it can be roughly schematized—but also in syntax, rhetoric, diction: all that goes into and comes from the tone of the poem. The fact that the six-word simple sentence "And I let the fish go" follows an eleven-line complex, compound sentence contributes to its effect of suddenness, simplicity, finality, and whatever else constitutes the flavor and resonance of the line that's harder to give a name to. It is as final as a final line can be without clanging the cymbals to announce the symphony is over. "The Fish" engages us, among other ways, through the syntax of the sentences falling across the predominantly three-beat lines. Frequently enjambed, occasionally interrupted by caesuras, the lines make a barely perceptible measure, with enough strategically placed strict iambic trimeter ("It hung a grunting weight"; "the little rented boat"; etc.) to keep, in Eliot's famous figure, "the ghost of some simple metre lurking behind the arras." As a consequence, the strange rhythm of the final line probably completes and disrupts the pattern simultaneously, with its four or almost-four beats, its perhaps-slightly-extended duration, and its open vowel rhyme (*rainbow/go:* one of three perfect rhymes in the long unrhymed poem). Its sound and rhythm amount to another formal contribution to the line's (and the poem's) mystery. I don't mean "mystification." We never need to ask what is happening in Bishop's poems. That would interfere with the poetry working on us. In absolute contrast to the *symbolistes* (and "modernist" poets influenced by them), the mystery in Bishop's poetry depends on clarity, the transparent surface of words—the simile is Wittgenstein's—"like the film on deep water."

Underneath the water, or inside it, is a dark gray flame:

> I have seen it over and over, the same sea, the same,
> slightly, indifferently swinging above the stones,
> icily free above the stones,
> above the stones and then the world.
> If you should dip your hand in,
> your wrist would ache immediately,
> your bones would begin to ache and your hand would burn
> as if the water were a transmutation of fire
> that feeds on stones and burns with a dark gray flame.

These lines, from near the end of "At the Fishhouses," *are* portentous and grand—wonderfully so, I think, because they are entirely prepared for. If they began the poem, we would probably be put off by their rhetoric. They would be stripped of the power of our assent patiently gathered from the solid dramatic scene and its various tonalities: her conversation with the old fisherman ("a friend of my grandfather"), her singing hymns to the seal, the "million Christmas trees . . . waiting for Christmas." But at the same time that Bishop is presenting funny, sad, mundane daily life in a wholly recognizable world, she gradually builds an undertone with the visual incantation of that ubiquitous silver (the sea, benches, lobster pots, masts, buildings, fish tubs, wheelbarrows, flies, fish scales, tree trunks, etc.) and with the repetition of the ominous, uncharacteristically unpunctuated series of adjectives that describe the sea: "Cold dark deep and absolutely clear." As in "The Fish," but more powerfully and profoundly, the speaker is repeatedly drawn back to the object, "the clear gray icy water"; at the climax (the beginning of which is quoted above), the pronouns shift from "I" to "you" to "we" as if the self flips and expands from the pressure of the water pulling her observation down into itself and out the other side to what it stands for, "what we imagine knowledge to be." But here observation does not keep or hold; "our knowledge" is "flowing, and flown." This well-worn idea still retains its poignancy because we *feel* it here in the heightened rhetoric enacting the transformation of all we have experienced so vividly in the given world of the poem, all that's calm, comforting, humorous and human swept away by time-the-destroyer in what is as close to an apocalypse as Bishop ever gets.

This grand sweep in "At the Fishhouses" is unique in Bishop's work, and it was characteristic of her not to repeat a subject or fixed form in the hundred or so poems she published. This conscious restraint makes all the more noticeable her almost compulsive repetition of a particular structural tic of turning the poem at the very end, often in the last line or half-line, in order to change what has preceded it, and change the whole poem on the second reading (there are many, many examples; "and you love me," the last half-line of "Insomnia," is one of the clearest and most effective). She may have first encountered this device in Herbert's "Decay" ("and all things burn"); it enables her to begin with an "absolute naturalness of tone" and still enact a "transmutation" of elements that turns them into poetry.

The openings of "The Fish," "At the Fishhouses," and "In the Waiting Room" are fairly representative:

I caught a tremendous fish
and held him beside the boat
half out of water, with my hook
fast in a corner of his mouth.

―――

Although it is a cold evening,
down by one of the fishhouses
an old man sits netting

―――

In Worcester, Massachusetts,
I went with Aunt Consuelo
to keep her dentist's appointment
and sat and waited for her
in the dentist's waiting room.

They could hardly be more plain and matter-of-fact. Structurally, they serve as the base metal for the later "transmutation." And this device of turning-the-poem-at-the-end is probably too consistently guided by reticence translated into technique. Maybe because Bishop was such a conscious artist, her work is most moving, at least to me, when she is not in her "right mind," when the poem admits what it resists and steps beyond the established range of decorum―if only implicitly, in terms of style. Of course, as at the end of "At the Fishhouses," these great moments are made possible by the shape and context of the whole, which is inseparable from the poet's reticence or the poem's decorum. "Shampoo" and "Insomnia," two of her rare love poems, work so well because the inherent power of the subject is boosted by its reticent treatment. As Sisela Bok says in *Secrets: On the Ethics of Concealment and Revelation*, "Making something secret gives it value. Indeed, a secret creates in us the sense of interior life." But a secret may also be the lifeblood of shame. In Bishop's best poems, this "sense of interior life" seems infinitely rich and yet embodied in the ordinary, visible world. "An ancient chill is rippling the dark brooks," she writes in the last line of "Cape Breton," three lines after one as plain and prosaic as "The birds keep on singing, a calf bawls, a bus starts." These are the two terminals that conduct the current, and undercurrent, in her poetry. When one is missing, invariably it's the "ancient chill," and there's no emotional charge. It is as if she's protecting herself from the world too much to uncover what draws her to it. We are left with a pleasant display of good manners.

The portentous diction and unusually heavy stresses and sound linkage of the last line of "Cape Breton," like the anaphora in the lines quoted from "At the Fishhouses," show the character of the language itself taking on the intensity of "transmutation." But, as I've tried to indicate, these moments do not and cannot exist in isolation, and depend on Bishop's "unique exactitude of detail" to engage us through language less intensely wrought but no less carefully used. She wrote about Moore's poetry in 1948:

> I do not understand the nature of the satisfaction a completely accurate description or imitation of anything at all can give, but apparently in order to produce it the imitation must be brief, or compact, and have at least the effect of being spontaneous. Even the best *trompe-l'oeil* paintings lack it, but I have experienced it in listening to the noise made by a four-year-old child who could imitate the sound of water running out of his bath. Long, fine, thorough passages of descriptive prose fail to produce it, but sometimes animal or bird masks at the Museum of Natural History give one (or the dances that once went with them might have been able to do) the same immediacy of identification one feels on reading about Miss Moore's
>
> > Small dog, going over the lawn, nipping the linen
> > and saying
> > that you have a badger
>
> or the butterfly that
>
> > flies off
> > diminishing like wreckage on the sea,
> > rising and falling easily.
>
> Does it come simply from her gift of being able to give herself up entirely to the object under contemplation, to feel in all sincerity

how it is to be *it*? From whatever the pleasure may be derived, it is certainly one of the greatest the work of Miss Moore gives us.

This is also one of the greatest pleasures the work of Miss Bishop gives us, even, I think, the primary pleasure insofar as it makes all others possible by establishing the context in which they can be felt. It seems analogous to what Bernard Berenson meant by "tactile values" in painting: we're given the "material significance" of the object so that it feels tangible to us. No one is better at this than Bishop. So many objects are rendered freshly in her poetry that even if it were nothing else it could stand as a manual for how to see. One of the many that has lodged in my memory comes near the end of "Roosters," when the "low light" of dawn "is floating / in the backyard, and gilding / from underneath / the broccoli, leaf by leaf." The "gilding from underneath"—a wording she may have discovered through the stricture and agency of the tercets—brings the dawn alive and makes us see how low and gradual its light is.

Bishop surely had to observe the dawn this closely before she could render it this vividly, but getting the shape of the "thing" right, so it would produce that "immediacy of identification," was usually a slow process. She apparently wrote a few of her poems at one sitting, such as the long ballad "The Burglar of Babylon," but Lowell told a story of seeing unfinished lines pasted on her bulletin board with one word changed and then another in months-long intervals between visits. She averaged a little more than two poems a year, split almost exactly between "fixed forms" and "free verse"—both of these terms, especially in her case, being misnomers. When her lines seem prosaic, it's usually due less to the irregularity of stress than to its relative lightness compared to the "unstressed" syllables in the line, but her meters and rhymes are invariably pushed, pulled, and loosened, and act as a subtle counterpoint to the natural flow of the sentence (whose primacy she signifies by capitalizing according to punctuation, not at the beginnings of lines). Her free verse is tightened so that it nearly meets her metrical verse at a kind of Platonic rhythmical mean, yet the two are used for distinctly different opportunities and effects. I've talked about the rhythm of the final line of "The Fish"; the last line of "In-

somnia" ("is now deep, and you love me") unquestionably breaks the
barely-established iambic trimeter pattern as it reveals the source of
the speaker's insomnia, that all along she has been bereft.

> The moon in the bureau mirror
> looks out a million miles
> (and perhaps with pride, at herself,
> but she never, never smiles)
> far and away beyond sleep, or
> perhaps she's a daytime sleeper.
>
> By the Universe deserted,
> *she*'d tell it to go to hell,
> and she'd find a body of water,
> or a mirror, on which to dwell.
> So wrap up care in a cobweb
> and drop it down the well
>
> into that world inverted
> where left is always right,
> where the shadows are really the body,
> where we stay awake all night,
> where the heavens are shallow as the sea
> is now deep, and you love me.

Bishop's *Collected Prose* consists of seventeen pieces, nine catego-
rized as reminiscences and eight as fiction (though there is very little
formal distinction between them), seven of which she didn't attempt
to print during her lifetime. Jarrell's criticism overwhelmingly applies:
most of the pieces are "just description." Except for "In the Village,"
"Efforts of Affection," and occasional paragraphs of other pieces, the
book is interesting to read only alongside her poetry to see how much
she gained from the form of verse, not only at individual moments,
but dramatically, in shaping the rendering of an object or incident.

There could be no clearer example of this than the last paragraph of
"The Country Mouse" set against "In the Waiting Room." Both deal
with her childhood experience of sudden self-identity as a human
being in a dentist's waiting room, but the pace and structure—the

modulation between the dramatic scene and the little girl's feelings—
are much more effective in the poem. "The Country Mouse" ends:

> After New Year's, Aunt Jenny had to go to the dentist, and asked
> me to go with her. She left me in the waiting room, and gave me a
> copy of the *National Geographic* to look at. It was still getting dark
> early, and the room had grown very dark. There was a big yellow
> lamp in one corner, a table with magazines, and an overhead
> chandelier of sorts. There were others waiting, two men and a
> plump middle-aged lady, all bundled up. I looked at the magazine
> cover—I could read most of the words—shiny, glazed, yellow
> and white. The black letters said: February 1918. A feeling of abso-
> lute and utter desolation came over me. I felt . . . *myself*. In a few
> days it would be my seventh birthday. I felt *I, I, I,* and looked at
> the three strangers in panic. I was *one* of them too, inside my
> scabby body and wheezing lungs. "You're in for it now," some-
> thing said. How had I got tricked into such a false position? I
> would be like that woman opposite who smiled at me so falsely
> every once in a while. The awful sensation passed, then it came
> back again. "You are you," something said. "How strange you are,
> inside looking out. You are not Beppo, or the chestnut tree, or
> Emma, you are *you* and you are going to be *you* forever." It was
> like coasting downhill, this thought, only much worse, and it
> quickly smashed into a tree. *Why* was I a human being?

And here's the middle of "In the Waiting Room":

> I said to myself: three days
> and you'll be seven years old.
> I was saying it to stop
> the sensation of falling off
> the round, turning world
> into cold, blue-black space.
> But I felt: you are an *I*,
> you are an *Elizabeth*,
> you are one of *them*.
> *Why* should you be one, too?

I scarcely dared to look
to see what it was I was.
I gave a sidelong glance
—I couldn't look any higher—
at shadowy gray knees,
trousers and skirts and boots
and different pairs of hands
lying under the lamps.
I knew that nothing stranger
had ever happened, that nothing
stranger could ever happen.

And the ending:

The waiting room was bright
and too hot. It was sliding
beneath a big black wave,
another, and another.

Then I was back in it.
The War was on. Outside,
in Worcester, Massachusetts,
were night and slush and cold,
and it was still the fifth
of February, 1918.

The strangeness of identity, of the accident of being human, becomes objective in the poem; place and time are cast as rigid, arbitrary, intersecting planes. We are immersed in the child's point of view, in her perception as well as her feelings: her feelings are dramatized in her perceptions. We are kept inside the waiting room (a pun, I think, Bishop intended), not taken outside by the clumsy simile of coasting downhill and smashing into a tree. The real strangeness is *not* having physically moved in actual space and historical time, at a moment of such great psychological passage. In the simplest way possible, this odd, particular, personal experience becomes by extension the reader's experience.

Bishop's *Complete Poems* are dated by the publisher 1927–1979: fifty-two years that span the Depression, World War Two, wars in Korea and Vietnam, the rise and fall of Hitler, the Holocaust, the postwar Communist witch hunt, the Civil Rights movement, the women's movement, the dropping of atomic bombs on Japan, and the build-up of nuclear weapons and the capacity for the world's annihilation, among other important historical events. Besides the setting of "In the Waiting Room" during World War One, Bishop makes not a single reference to any of these in her poetry. Self-described as a socialist, she nonetheless said she was "opposed to political thinking as such for writers." It may be a matter of conviction if this bespeaks a limitation to her work, but certainly the function of poetry for Bishop was personal and not cultural, even if writing itself was a public act.

Maybe the catastrophic history of Bishop's lifetime does enter her poetry in the assumption behind lines like "—the little that we get for free, / the little of our earthly trust" and "(A yesterday I find impossible to lift)," in the feelings of the writer about being alive—"awful, but cheerful"—that manifested itself in the tone of her poetry. This tone becomes noticeably darker in her last volume, *Geography III*, but unlike Yeats she was never impelled to "remake" herself over her fifty-two years of work, maybe because from the beginning she was so happily married to her technique.

"We think in generalities," wrote Whitehead, "but live in detail." Is there a more fundamental reason why good writing depends on the creation of an accessible world? Details may be rendered differently from poem to poem and poet to poet, but in Bishop's best work the close weave between the actual and imagined, the visible and invisible, becomes a rich fabric so palpable it makes us want to pick it up and hold it in our hands.

FLAUBERT IN FLORIDA

The unusual technical variety of Donald Justice's poetry issues like Bishop's from his consistent refusal to repeat himself, although his rich refusals are indicative of a very different temperament than hers, woven into the fabric of his poetry like "God in the universe, present everywhere and visible nowhere," a temperament as relentless as Flaubert's in its insistence on perfect objectivity. Since Justice's first poems, the unmistakable impression of that famous signature has been just beneath his own: the painstaking search for *le mot juste,* that particular Flaubertian mixture of razor intelligence, cold eye, disaffection, and hermeticism. Justice would agree with Flaubert that "Poetry is as precise as geometry," but would probably note with irony that we now know that even basic axioms can only be proved within closed systems. Each of Justice's poems is a closed system. Formal limits, conventional or invented, are in his view connected to the nature of language. Only by means of such limits can a world which is always threatening to dissolve be focused and "fixed"—as he says of the effect of meter—by achieving form (it would be characteristic if he chose the word "fixed" in this context for both of its meanings: "stabilized" *and* "rectified").

At the same time, a formal exercise is sterile unless it uncovers some rich, unavoidable secret. Flaubert kept a stuffed, green parrot on his writing desk to remind himself of the irrational—at the same writing desk on which he composed the sentence "Poetry is as precise as geometry." For both Flaubert and Justice, the finished work does not resolve this paradox so much as embody it, as if concurrent, conflicting desires for the wholly mysterious and the wholly comprehensible can be satisfied only in and by the work itself.

Justice's green parrot appears in "Tales from a Family Album," caged but alive—fed by an "aunt" who, the speaker says, never "overcame her fears, yet missed no feeding, / Thrust in the crumbs with thimbles on her fingers." This is the sort of elaborate literary joke Justice delights in, and it sometimes generates lines and even whole poems. In "The Mild Despair of Tremayne," "mordancies of the armchair" is obviously a take-off of Stevens's "complacencies of the peignoir"; in "Variations on a Text by Vallejo," Donald Justice dies in Miami on a sunny Sunday instead of César Vallejo in Paris on a rainy Thursday. And in "The Summer Anniversaries" (recast completely in Justice's *Selected Poems* from the opening poem in his first volume), when the poet-at-age-ten exclaims "O brave new planet!—/ And with such music in it," we are probably expected to understand that, in contrast to Miranda in *The Tempest* ("O brave new world, / That hath such people in't!"), this child *prefers* music.

But the allusiveness pervading Justice's poems is less an act of criticism (as it was for Pound) or a structural principle (as it was for Eliot) than simply a way of working, of getting the poem onto the page, for a writer who is "loaded down with selfconsciousness." This description of Justice is his own, from an interview published in *The Ohio Review;* he talks there about this way of working as "borrowing the voice":

> Borrowing the voice allows me, it seems, to speak of myself more directly, more objectively because the voice is not mine. Not simply mine. Probably more than other poets I know, I play games in my poems (as I do in my life), and one of the unwritten rules of the game for me, as I like it played, is that you can risk this much personality or that much confession if the voice is promised to be that of someone else to start with. Even without my recognizing it at the time of writing, that may be one of the reasons I can get pretty literary in my choice of subjects, in taking off from other people's texts. There is something in the works of others, I

suppose, that gets to me personally, that affords me another perspective, the objectivity and distance I like, so that it is as if I could say to myself, let me use his experience as an image of my own, and I won't have to use mine. But using this turns out to be another experience for me, so it really *will* be mine in the end.

This doesn't account for all, or nearly all, of Justice's poems—in his most recent work, he has written most often about private experiences, past and present, with his usual detachment yet without "borrowing the voice." But the passage illustrates the paradoxical cast of mind ("the objectivity and distance I like") that determines how his poems are made. And they are, above all, *made,* whether from their external forms inward, or from their emotional centers outward (as in the poems Justice starts with another poet's "experience as an image of [his] own"). The limitations of this way of working are obvious, but if as a consequence we rarely feel that "he *had* to write about the subject he took, and in that way" (one of Eliot's main criteria for "a great writer"), the poet's distance may be compensated by the poem's immediacy. Given ideal skill, a poet implicitly argues for a particular kind of poetry by writing his poems the way he does, but he also writes the way he does simply because he hasn't any other choice. Stevens put it better when he said, "I write the way I do not because it pleases me, but because no other way pleases me." The distinctive character of Justice's style—its unusual lucidity and perfect decorum—may be his response to his temperament as well as a reflection of it. How can a person for whom "emotion tends to disappear when much show is made of it" (another self-description) still write poetry? Justice's style is his answer to this question.

This, then, is Justice's signature, too: the poet's emotion is withheld while the poem's material is presented. The opposite has often been true in American poetry since 1959, the *annus mirabilis* of confessional poetry with Lowell's *Life Studies* and Snodgrass's *Heart's Needle,* and Plath's *Ariel* soon to follow. Justice and Snodgrass were students at Iowa during the fifties, and Lowell taught there briefly. *Heart's Needle,* Snodgrass's first volume, won the Pulitzer Prize in 1960; Justice's first volume, *The Summer Anniversaries,* appeared the same year. It shows

Justice writing, if anything, *against* the confessional impulse, as he has ever since. The passion animating Justice's work has always been a passionate restraint, even a passion *for* restraint. In this way also it resembles Bishop's, but Justice tends much more to irony, which can in one mood turn bitter (see "Sonatina in Green"), and, in his dominant mood, he is much more attracted to possibilities for menace. Like Bishop for most of her life, Justice has been known as a "craftsman" and "a poet's poet." His poems invite this, as if, like some people, they would rather be respected than loved. At first glance, they may appear "cold," "traditional," or, as an acquaintance of mine described them, "sturdy"—to prefer modest accomplishment to ambitious failure. This is not endearing to a Romantic age. Like *Madame Bovary*, Justice's poetry goes to a great deal of trouble not to ask the reader to complete it. He tells us, twice, in "Poem": "This poem is not addressed to you," and, moreover, "it does not matter what you think" (there is a negation in almost every line). Not exactly a Whitmanian embrace.

Yet Justice's relentless insistence on clarity, on realizing the subject within the frame of the poem, amounts to a consideration of the reader, which to my mind is the greatest consideration. In a critical atmosphere that celebrates varieties of opacity as innovations, Justice's style, were it a matter of choice, would represent an act of moral courage. If this style proceeds from traditional assumptions about language, it nonetheless may make new poetry by mining old, rich veins and by fusing alloys of old and new, of English and European traditions.

Ingmar Bergman, whose films were a springboard for one of Justice's poems ("A Dancer's Life"), once said in an interview that the best camera angle is usually the one where the audience doesn't notice the camera. Justice certainly aims for such transparency, to present the subject seemingly without his intervention in (as Coleridge put it) "the best words in the best order." As a consequence, each word is required to have a fresh, rational use and placement, and decorum and wit are thereby elevated to major poetic virtues. And the worst of Justice's poetry suffers from "virtuosity," never from other common contemporary maladies of sloppiness, overwriting, inflation, sentimentality, obscurity, or tin ear. When Justice's poems fail, it is usually because they are eviscerated by self-conscious irony, mannerism, and literary poses of spiritual exhaustion that derive ultimately from the poetry of Flaubert's contemporaries and have already resurfaced in every possible guise in English poetry over the last hundred years. As the graffito says, ennui is boring. And as Eudora Welty says in her beautiful essay on Henry Green, "Virtuosity, unless it move the heart, goes at the head of the whole parade to dust." Adding immediately, "With Henry Green we always come back to this: this work is so moving." The extraordinary distillation that can be the main virtue of Justice's style leaves nothing for us to care about when the subject is too removed or attenuated or literary to begin with.

Consequently, Justice's poems are best when it does seem that "*he* had to write about the subject he took, and in that way" (switching Eliot's emphasis from *had* to *he*): when his style seems a discipline to contain his urgency, as if (as in Eliot's poetry) the powerful emotion aroused by the subject had to be powerfully muted in order to be objectively realized. These subjects, invariably, are a challenge to Justice's control, because of their richness or mystery, or—*almost* despite himself—his personal investment in them.

Here is one of the earliest (and shortest) of these poems, from *The Summer Anniversaries,* dating from about 1959:

A Map of Love

Your face more than others' faces
Maps the half-remembered places
I have come to while I slept—
Continents a dream had kept
Secret from all waking folk
Till to your face I awoke,
And remembered then the shore,
And the dark interior.

This is the closest thing to a love poem in Justice's *Selected Poems*—the only other "beloved" directly addressed is a dressmaker's dummy—

although there are other poems about sexual love, most often treated ironically. There's no irony in "A Map of Love," even if the poem begins with a characteristic qualification or deflation ("more than others' faces") that will be the business of the rest of the poem to overcome. This sort of deflation is the given when Justice picks up his pen; here it is explicit rather than assumed, which may account in part for this poem's effectiveness. The beloved's presence is barely felt, but the poem is not about her—it's about what she provokes, what takes place in the internal territory of the speaker's psyche. Hence the title (revised—and improved—from "Love's Map"), which is the governing trope.

Although this conceit is inventive enough, and its handling graceful enough, the main pleasure of the poem comes, at least to me, from how it presents its information in one sentence draped across trochaic tetrameter couplets. The poetry is more in this, the poem's enactment—the relationship of syntax, rhythm, and content—than in its paraphrasable ideas. "Your face" in the sixth line, for example, causes one of the few disjunctions between metrical and rhetorical stress in the poem, and we feel it as a slight dissonance, a subconscious emphasis, at an important moment in the drama. Marvell showed how the tetrameter couplet could be used in a serious poem by enjambing frequently; Justice does this, too, and in addition truncates the last six lines to seven syllables each, so that he's not locked into using feminine rhymes (e.g., *faces/places*), which in couplets tend after a while to become comic. The two middle rhyming pairs (*slept/kept, folk/ awoke*) have a hard, clipped sound, which sets us up for another variation at the end (*shore/interior*), a soft, half-rhyme on the final, weakly stressed syllable. This is Justice's main currency: subtle effects solidly based in the arrangement of the language, the organization of the poem. Metrically, the last line consists of two weaker stresses flanking two strong ones, again a slight variation within the established pattern of a four-stress line in which the first and last stresses are at least as strong as the others. The syntax of the sentence, besides organizing the elements of the plot, acquires a clarity and ease at the end which is in contrast with the knots and inversion in the middle. The last line is like Yeats's click of the closing box; it wants to gather and culminate all that has preceded it, and it does. The speaker's shock of recognition is dramatized by the syntax; what is discovered (in the Platonic sense, "remembered") comes last: "the dark interior." We not only understand this shock, we feel it, literally, in the variations of sound, rhythm, and syntax.

This feeling is fused by the words of the poem to our understanding, our "memory" of the experience of having discovered "the dark interior" of ourselves through another person. Such effects may be most easily traced in poems in fixed forms because the pattern of rhythm and rhyme is roughly identifiable, but the sound and syntax of free verse must work analogously or it probably isn't verse at all. The extraordinary palpability of Justice's poems derives as much from the clarity of their shapes as of their subjects, but subject and shape are inextricable in language that simultaneously has sound, syntax, and meaning. Since we pay attention primarily to meaning, the sound and syntax subliminally influence the way we receive it, but the sound and syntax—separately and in combination—also make complicated, protean shapes of their own that the reader may not attend to, but which work on him nonetheless. For Justice, at least in 1964, a poem by its nature calls for "a different sort of attention on the part of both writer and reader":

> If in a novel the great event is likely to be a death or wedding, in a poem it may well be a sentence, a line, a phrase, or just possibly a single word.

This was the sort of attention encouraged by New Criticism. If current academic criticism is any indication, such attention has almost disappeared from the reading (if not the writing) of poetry. The poets included in *New Poets of England and America* (1957), mostly born in the twenties, were brought up on the assumptions of New Criticism, but almost all of them discarded these assumptions as "academic" within a few years of the anthology's publication. Although Justice was also influenced by the proliferation of translation in the sixties, and himself edited an anthology of *Contemporary French Poetry,* he never underwent the complete turnaround of a Merwin or Rich. Reading Justice's *Selected Poems* in chronological sequence, as it's happily arranged, no careful reader would confuse a poem from the late sixties with one written ten years earlier or ten years later; the volume as a whole presents even Justice's poetic development with unusual clarity. Yet the attention to "a sentence, a line, a phrase, or just possibly a single word," which he could have learned from Yvor Winters at Stanford in 1948, is the constant in Justice's *Selected Poems* from the oldest poems to the most recent.

What makes the book interesting as a volume, however, is the sense of Justice's testing his assumptions and experimenting with them, from poem to poem. So, if in 1964 (in an essay called "The Writing of Poetry," also quoted above) he wrote:

> In a good short poem a fine sense of relations among its parts is felt, word connecting with word, line with line: as with a spider web, touch it at any part and the whole structure responds.

—which could be an excerpt from the most orthodox New Critical text (and is surely the structural principle of "A Map of Love")—at about the same time he could also write a poem which challenges such structural principles:

The Suicides

If we recall your voices
As softer now, it's only
That they must have drifted back

A long way to have reached us
Here, and upon such a wind
As crosses the high passes.

Nor does the blue of your eyes
(Remembered) cast much light on
The page ripped from the tablet.

~

Once there in the labyrinth,
You were safe from your reasons.
We stand, now, at the threshold,

Peering in, but the passage,
For us, remains obscure: the
Corridors are still bloody.

~

What you meant to prove you have
Proved—we did not care for you
Nearly enough. Meanwhile the

Bay was preparing herself
To receive you, the for once
Wholly adequate female

To your dark inclinations;
Under your care the pistol
Was slowly learning to flower

In the desired explosion,
Disturbing the careful part
And the briefly recovered

Fixed smile of a forgotten
Triumph; deep within the black
Forest of childhood that tree

Was already rising which,
With the length of your body,
Would cast the double shadow.

~

The masks by which we knew you
Have been torn from you. Even
Those mirrors, to which always

You must have turned to confide,
Cannot have recognized you,
Stripped, as you were, finally.

At the end of your shadow
There sat another, waiting,
Whose back was always to us.

~

When the last door had been closed,
You watched, inwardly raging,
For the first glimpse of your selves
Approaching, jangling their keys.

Musicians of the black keys,
At last you compose yourselves.
We hear the music raging
Under the lids we have closed.

If the overall structure of "The Suicides" does not seem much like
a spider web, the poem nonetheless makes as much sense as "Map of
Love," even if sense does derive largely from the "relations among its
parts." The conceit of "A Map of Love" causes the sequence of images
to acquire a kind of momentum like that in problem solving, and, in
retrospect, we see that their order and relationship is fixed and necessary (map-shore-interior). In "The Suicides," the sections seem to
be in an appropriate order, and we especially feel the "lastness" of the
last section, but the images from section to section don't lock into a
connecting logic of their own. The high passes of section one, for
example, have nothing to do with the mirrors of section four, and, in
fact, a main source of pleasure in the poem is the multiplicity and
variety of its figures.

Then how does the poem hold together? There are "spider webs"
in "The Suicides," but they are within the sections and not among
them, so this represents only what might be called the poem's second-
ary structure. The effect of this sectioning is to let in more air, which
is sorely needed because of the nature of the subject. And the subject,
as it turns out, is less the suicides, the people who died, than the reaction of the living, the opacity of self-destruction. In spite of their
differences, "The Suicides" and "A Map of Love" are identical in this

one way: just as the presence of the beloved is distilled in the earlier poem, the suicides are barely felt because the poem is not about them but about the connection of their act of self-destruction to the living.

This is also the connection that holds the poem together. The grace and ingenuity of "The Suicides" becomes apparent when one notices the placement of the we-you pronouns, and the variety of ways they are yoked, syntactically and dramatically. This address—of a representative "we" to an equally, if oppositely, representative "you"—pervades the poem, but Justice modulates it continuously, causing it to be absorbed into little dramas, putting a little more weight now upon the "we" (as in the second section), now upon the "you" (as in the third). As a structuring device, this allows much more range than the development of a single conceit. The poem seems at once various and unified, fluid and solid.

Each section of "The Suicides" begins with the we-you address, cast in terms of drama or statement or some combination of the two. This is necessary structural work, but never seems obtrusive or repetitious:

> If *we* recall *your* voices
> As softer now . . .

> ———

> Once there in the labyrinth,
> *You* were safe from your reasons.
> *We* stand, now, at the threshold. . . .

> ———

> What *you* meant to prove *you* have
> Proved—*we* did not care for *you*
> Nearly enough.

> ———

> The masks by which *we* knew *you*
> Have been torn from *you*.

Part of our pleasure in the poem comes from the variety, efficiency, and inventiveness with which this structural work is accomplished, whether we are aware of its being accomplished or not. We're reminded at the beginning of each section that the poem is addressed to the suicides, and this focuses each section's elaboration of its figures while these elaborations keep the focus on the suicides from being unbearably constricted. The result is a pattern of departure and return, a movement in the mind thinking about the suicides, away and back, the response preferred and the one compelled.

The last section is a kind of coda to this movement. It's a formal *tour de force*, the end words of the first stanza mirrored in the second: closed, raging, yourselves, keys; keys, yourselves, raging, closed. The form mimics the balance and opposition of the "we" and "you" throughout the poem. The first stanza is given to the suicides, and is a wholly dramatic rendering of their first moments after death. And the second stanza belongs to the "we," the living, once again addressing the suicides (although for the first time with an epithet: "Musicians of the black keys"). Drama and direct address, the representative "you" and the representative "we," departure and return—the opposites previously combined in the poem are here isolated, presented in separate stanzas. Yet they are linked through the form, the end words locking into place a closure that the previous sections avoid. The connection between the "we" and the "you," the living and the dead, is more felt than spoken, and felt primarily through the poem's form and structure. And of course it's no accident that the emotional climax of the poem occurs at a moment when the form is most disciplined.

"The Suicides" is one of Justice's earliest poems in syllabics, which he used frequently in the mid-sixties, and in which he did some of his best work ("The Suicides," "The Tourist from Syracuse," "Hands") and, curiously, some of his worst ("In the Greenroom," "At a Rehearsal of Uncle Vanya," "To the Hawks"). The former group are in seven-syllable lines, and the latter in five-syllable, and it's as if the shorter line is too constricted. The syllabic line, even as Justice uses it, has no prosodic identity in English. It doesn't provide a measure (since the duration of each syllable is variable) but simply an arbitrary restriction to an otherwise free verse. Justice no doubt became interested in syllabics through his translation of French—in which the syllable *is* the measure—and it may have given him a way to write a line that is closer to speech than did his earlier metrical line, on his way to writing free verse with its own rhythmical identity.

A good book could be written on how Justice uses free verse that would also be a manual of prosody for contemporary poetry. Invariably, the line acts as a tensioning device against the syntax of the sentence, which both discloses its prose rhythm and makes it into something else. One of the best examples, "Men at Forty," also dates from the mid-sixties, when Justice was working primarily with the syllabic line. The poem consists of five stanzas and five sentences, and it gives me great pleasure to watch how the sentences fall into the stanzas and across them, and how the sentence is cut on the phrase to uncover its rhythm and cut against the phrase for the sake of the poetry.

Men at Forty

Men at forty
Learn to close softly
The doors to rooms they will not be
Coming back to.

At rest on a stair landing,
They feel it
Moving beneath them now like the deck of a ship,
Though the swell is gentle.

And deep in mirrors
They rediscover
The face of the boy as he practices tying
His father's tie there in secret

And the face of that father,
Still warm with the mystery of lather.
They are more fathers than sons themselves now.
Something is filling them, something

That is like the twilight sound
Of the crickets, immense,
Filling the woods at the foot of the slope
Behind their mortgaged houses.

The basic prosodic principle at work here is one Justice learned from his lifetime study of meter: the establishment of pattern and variation on it. The first two lines must be cut on the phrase in order for the third to have any effect cut against it (reinforced by the triplet rhyme: *forty/softly/be*). And this applies to the first two sentences each snugly fitting a stanza, a pattern varied by the last three sentences in the last three stanzas. The breaks between stanzas three and four and stanzas four and five also seem articulate, almost part of the content, as does the fact that the statement embedded in the fourth stanza is one sentence and one line.

"Men at Forty" has all the clarity of shape of the most formal poem because it *is* a most formal poem. Justice's most effective writing has often taken the form of free verse because it has caused an even greater fidelity to the subject. This is what I mean by "palpability": it is as if the thing itself were given to us to hold in our hands: it is a quality of lucidity in the choice of words and their organization, the language honed to a fine transparency.

> And the sun will be bright then on the dark glasses of strangers
> And in the eyes of a few friends from my childhood
> And of the surviving cousins by the graveside,
> While the diggers, standing apart, in the still shade of the palms,
> Rest on their shovels, and smoke,
> Speaking in Spanish softly, out of respect.
>
> ———
>
> The breast of Mary Something, freed from a white swimsuit,
> Damp, sandy, warm; or Margery's, a small caught bird
>
> ———
>
> And here comes one to repair himself at the mirror,
> Patting down damp, sparse hairs, suspiciously still black,
> Poor bantam cock of a man, jaunty at one a.m., perfumed,
>   undiscourageable.

The tone, of course, varies, and the kinds of "things" presented, and the uses made of them. But, as in "Men at Forty," this quality of

Justice's style seems to be what allows him to bring over into language something we did not have before.

Like so many of Justice's poems, the *donnée* of "Men at Forty" can be traced to a literary source; in this case, to Wallace Stevens's "Le Monocle de Mon Oncle":

> If men at forty will be painting lakes
> The ephemeral blues must merge for them in one,
> The basic slate, the universal hue.
> There is a substance in us that prevails.

The figure of Flaubert probably shades into the large figure of Wallace Stevens in the background of Justice's work, and it would be hard not to be overshadowed by it. Justice shares many of Stevens's beliefs, and lack of them. Poetry is certainly "a conscious activity" for Justice, and it was probably from Stevens that he learned that poems can conceal as well as reveal. But one does not feel in Justice's work that it is "a sanction of life," except perhaps a life in memory. The "Supreme Fiction," the "magnificent fury," the "blessed rage for order" that animates Stevens's poetry at its best—in short, the ambition in his work to encompass life and even to replace it—is not part of Justice's temperament or intention. This may be only Justice's reading of history or literary history, but it informs the poems he has written. As he says in "Homage to the Memory of Wallace Stevens": "The *the* has become an *a*." However, those who have read Justice as a Stevens epigone have read him badly.

"Men at Forty" is also illuminated by what Justice does not take from "Le Monocle de Mon Oncle": namely, the subject of a sexual relationship in middle age. This absence is an undercurrent in Justice's poem, the absence of anyone else except in memory, the absence of connection to other human beings.

And this, I think, is Justice's main subject, although most often it appears only implicitly (characteristically enough) in poems about memory, about an almost Edenic childhood. The child is "happily ignored," and knows "the pleasures of certain solitudes," but Justice's myth of childhood is pervaded by a sense of community, of a proper, workable, social role not available to the adult *poète maudit,* even a tenured *poète maudit.* What the childhood actually was—and a number of Justice's poems refer to a serious childhood illness—is less important to him than the fact of its being remembered, because the very act of remembering for Justice is a gesture of identity in a dissolving world. His poetry is above all a poetry of isolation, composed in exile, most often—not so paradoxically—with the help of other poems, knowingly, sometimes even "rationally" (while employing "chance methods"), always moving toward the consolations of memory and form.

I think my favorite poem of Justice's is my favorite because this implicit condition is made explicit and is written about directly. It is, in this sense, both uncharacteristic and central to his work. The poem was composed as one of a pair of companion pieces (the other is entitled "Absences"), and it "borrows the voice" of César Vallejo's "Agape." Both of these contexts may enrich our reading of the poem, but I think I begin to see the heart of Justice's work when it is stripped of them:

Presences

Everyone, everyone went away today.
They left without a word, and I think
I did not hear a single goodbye today.

And all that I saw was someone's hand, I think,
Thrown up out there like the hand of someone drowning,
But far away, too far to be sure what it was or meant.

No, but I saw how everything had changed
Later, just as the light had; and at night
I saw that from dream to dream everything changed.

And those who might have come to me in the night,
The ones who did come back but without a word,
All those I remembered passed through my hands like clouds—

Clouds out of the south, familiar clouds—
But I could not hold onto them, they were drifting away,
Everything going away in the night again and again.

"How hard it is to live with what you know and nothing else"—this
line is Camus's, and one from which Justice would surely excise the
first two words. But it begins to describe the stark discipline of
Justice's poetry and the severe limits of its spirit, and tells me why
I sometimes find it moving even if, as he has said, he would not
have it so.

BETWEEN SCYLLA AND CHARYBDIS

This is one of the poems by Stanley Kunitz I love the most:

My Sisters

Who whispered, souls have shapes?
So has the wind, I say.
But I don't know.
I only feel things blow.

I had two sisters once
with long black hair
who walked apart from me
and wrote the history of tears.
Their story's faded with their names,
but the candlelight they carried,
like dancers in a dream,
still flickers on their gowns
as they bend over me
to comfort my night-fears.

Let nothing grieve you,
Sarah and Sophia.
Shush, shush, my dears,
now and forever.

The poem is beyond comment, or underneath it, at least in the language of criticism, which is "a kind of translation," as Eudora

Welty says, "like a headphone we can clamp on at the U.N. when they are speaking the Arabian tongue." "My Sisters" resists this translation exceptionally well because its Arabic is silence—the silences of the past, of lost time, death, and eternity. These are different silences, and one of the accomplishments of the poem is that it differentiates them. It makes them distinct and present and felt as such, and then gathers them into that tender, heartrending final imperative—"Shush, shush"—a comforting gesture, a wish for silence as relief from sadness or grief or a child's night fears (and so calling back to stanza two), a wish for silence as relief from frailty and mortality. Just as the past becomes present (through the agency of "the candlelight they carried" that "still flickers"), and the comforted finally becomes the comforter (and vice-versa), this last gesture transforms the preceding silences into one silence that includes not only the poem's characters but also its readers. At least this reader. It makes me feel the intimate texture of the simple, inexhaustible fact that, as Kunitz wrote in an essay, "we are living and dying at the same time."

The way it does this is primarily nondiscursive, through structure, movement, music, and drama. "The best part" of a poem, Frost said, is "the unspoken part." Almost all of "My Sisters" is unspoken in this sense, like Hardy's "During Wind and Rain," which so exceeds its commonplace idea (that human beings are mortal) by embodying its emotional truth in structure and rhythm, refrain and variation, in the voice that speaks the first five lines of each stanza and begins the poem "They sing their dearest songs" and the voice that invariably answers in the last two lines of each stanza and closes the poem "Down their carved names the rain-drop ploughs." Here's the poem:

> They sing their dearest songs—
> He, she, all of them—yea,
> Treble and tenor and bass,
>   And one to play;
> With the candles mooning each face. . . .
>   Ah, no; the years O!
> How the sick leaves reel down in throngs!

They clear the creeping moss—
Elders and juniors—aye,
Making the pathways neat
    And the garden gay;
And they build a shady seat. . . .
    Ah, no; the years, the years;
See, the white storm-birds wing across!

They are blithely breakfasting all—
Men and maidens—yea,
Under the summer tree,
    With a glimpse of the bay,
While pet fowl come to the knee. . . .
    Ah, no; the years O!
And the rotten rose is ript from the wall.

They change to a high new house,
He, she, all of them—aye,
Clocks and carpets and chairs
    On the lawn all day,
And brightest things that are theirs. . . .
    Ah, no; the years, the years;
Down their carved names the rain-drop ploughs.

"My Sisters" has two voices, too, but their function and relationship are very different from those of Hardy's poem. The voice of the
first stanza frames the rest of "My Sisters" like one of Vermeer's half-
opened windows that filter and admit the light in which everything
appears at once tangible and numinous. It is a voice out of nowhere,
from the wilderness of inner space, not the same "I" that speaks the
second and third stanzas but given terrestrial life by that "I." "There
is an aspect of one's existence that has nothing to do with personal
identity, but that falls away from self, blends into the natural universe," Kunitz wrote in *a Kind of Order, a Kind of Folly*. This is the
first "I" of "My Sisters," appropriately distinguished by italics from
the personal "I" who has memories and affections and a life in time.

One of the dramatic undercurrents in the poem is their blending together "into the natural universe" of silence.

The first line of the poem—"*Who whispered, souls have shapes?*"—sets the tone. It echoes in my ear "Who said, 'Peacock Pie'?" the beginning of a strange, wonderful poem by a strange, sometimes wonderful poet, Walter de la Mare, who is still much loved in England and now mostly unread in the United States. De la Mare's is another poem in two voices, one that questions and one that replies, a mechanical arrangement meant to go nowhere, unlike "My Sisters," which moves great distances gracefully "like dancers in a dream." "My Sisters," in fact, is a miracle of movement, traveling from the impersonal undervoice of the opening to the intimate direct address of the ending, invariably immediate and increasingly dramatic. Is this movement over the fluid three-beat lines marked by the irregular rhymes and half-rhymes what makes the form feel like a membrane that can barely contain an overwhelming grief and sweetness? The way the three-beat line is used is a joy to look at closely. The second sentence of the second stanza, besides organizing the dramatic sequence and lodging the dramatic image so it won't be forgotten, is cut into lines of rhythmical beauty and function. "Like dancers in a dream" is the pivotal line of the six-line sentence. Its return to the strict iambic trimeter, after the rhythmical variation of the previous three lines, physiologically and psychologically brings the line home. Its satisfaction of the rhythmical expectation mounting since the previous strict iambic trimeter ("who walked apart from me") is bonded to its semantic content, and the image of the "dancers in a dream" thereby acquires the authority of that satisfaction. "Like dancers in a dream" also reestablishes the ground beat, the rhythmical context for the lines following it. "Still flickers on their gowns"—another iambic trimeter, but less insistently so—reinforces the metrical pattern, except unlike the previous three lines it isn't end-stopped, a subtle variation but enough with the line's slightly increased duration to loosen the rhythm just enough for what follows. In the next line, when the second beat occurs before we expect it to—"as they *bend* over me"—the moment takes on terrific emphasis, even if (especially if) it is registered subconsciously while we are attending to the drama, the meaning of the words. The gesture of bending becomes felt as it is described; it is not merely referred to but rendered.

Also, the subconscious rhythmical effect is so powerful at that moment it keeps us locked in the remembered scene to a degree that makes the surprising move into the direct address after the stanza break seem simple and natural. This kind of pivot or "turn"—what Petrarch called the "volta" between the octave and sestet of the sonnet—is one of the pleasures of poetic structures, and there are all sorts of turns in all sorts of poems, but this one, because of its solid grounding and imaginative wildness, seems to me inspired. The stanza break is used to move to the present for this address to the dead sisters: "Let nothing grieve you, / Sarah and Sophia." And, by saying their names, the story that "had faded with their names" is restored. They are memorialized (one of the oldest functions of poetry): the sisters are thereby given life, as in a ritual of the dead, at least for the rhythmical time of this poem. Their silence is shaped and, in the poem's last line, accepted and honored.

A good deal could be written about how the final stanza uses the established iambic trimeter to depart from it, but I want to look at only two lines, both examples of foreshortening but of different kinds. The first line—"Let nothing grieve you"—has three beats but a syllable missing in a strategic position in the final foot. The unexpected silence extends the long vowel of "grieve." Because of the metrical pattern, the word literally must be given more time than it normally takes to say it, just as the syllable "you" acquires a stronger stress than it would have in conversation. If there were an unstressed syllable between "grieve" and "you" (for example, "Let nothing grieve for you"), the glide of the long *e* wouldn't require such extension because the sound would be encased in the iambic trimeter. The sound would be shorter in the stricter meter. As it is, the held note makes an affecting music. It emphasizes the word, its music redoubling its meaning and making its meaning the reader's physical experience.

And the final line of the poem, working within and against the metrical grid, is even more effective and affecting: "Now and forever." Period. Two stresses and a feminine ending. In the ensuing silence after the final, unstressed syllable, after all those three-beat lines, the third stress never comes. Its absence is tangible, as if the silence itself were stressed, an endless incompletion, a longing for something missing, something lost.

The wealth of mystery in the poem, a good part of which is acquired through its rhythm and music, is not obscured by the slightest mystification. Its depths are discovered and displayed in a language simple and clear. Kunitz himself said in the *Paris Review* interview: "I dream of an art so transparent you can look through and see the world." He surely has accomplished this, and much more, in "My Sisters."

As much as a young poet could learn about writing poetry from Stanley Kunitz's poems, he or she could learn about the vocation of poetry from his prose. The book to mark his eightieth birthday appropriately included poems and essays. But his life with poetry has not been confined to writing. For Kunitz, poetry is a spiritual discipline, a way of being and of knowing oneself and the world, and he has purposefully presented himself as an example in a century when it has probably never been harder to live a poet's vocation and never been easier to cultivate a poet's "career," pathetic as such a career is next to those valued by corporate society. In this regard, although his style was initially suffused with Hopkins and the Metaphysical Poets, the figure of John Keats in his "vale of soul-making" has been Kunitz's main spiritual guide. In "The Modernity of Keats," first published in 1964, he wrote that Keats's "technique was not an aggregate of mechanical skills, but a form of spiritual testimony." And a decade later this observation was recast as Kunitz's central assumption in the foreword to *A Kind of Order, a Kind of Folly:*

> One of my unshakable convictions has been that poetry is more than a craft, important as the craft may be: it is a vocation, a passionate enterprise, rooted in human sympathies and aspirations.

Theoretically, it may appear that this vocation could be a private affair between the poet and his or her own soul, as it was for Emily Dickinson and for Hopkins, though in the latter case this was not entirely by choice. Hopkins wrote to his friend Dixon in 1878:

What I do regret is the loss of recognition belonging to the work itself. For as to every moral act, being right or wrong, there belongs, of the nature of things, reward or punishment, so to every form perceived by the mind belongs, of the nature of things, admiration or the reverse.

And, later in the same letter, more from the gut than from the Jesuit: "Disappointment and humiliation embitter the heart and make an aching in the very bones."

How many poets have sooner or later been poisoned by this bitterness? From the desire and need for an audience, disappointment and humiliation and worse have come. Even if this desire and need is expunged from the poet's heart, "art is social in origin" (as Jane Ellen Harrison says bluntly in *Ancient Art and Ritual*), and poetry still retains its fundamental social character, even when the society of which it's a product does not much care about it. In response to such neglect, poetry has often become hermetic, opaque, precious, or prosaic; it can become difficult (as Eliot said it *must* be in this century), like a child suffering from lack of attention. It can refuse to give pleasure, even to the poet who writes it. And the figure of the poet may become the *poète maudit*—Gérard de Nerval walking his lobster on a leash and hanging himself with a shoelace—dandified, flippant, and doomed, as in the wretched incarnation of Delmore Schwartz writing an essay entitled "The Vocation of the Poet in the Modern World":

> In the unpredictable and fearful future that awaits civilization, the poet must be prepared to be alienated and indestructible. He must dedicate himself to poetry, although no one else seems likely to read what he writes: he must be indestructible as a poet until he is destroyed as a human being.

In the absence of an audience, is the only choice killing the poetry or killing the poet? It's instructive and moving to watch how poets have tried to negotiate this Scylla and Charybdis in their lives and ideas and work. In his 1800 preface to *Lyrical Ballads,* Wordsworth internalizes the conflict between the poet and a culture that has abandoned him, because his original social function is served by more efficient institutions and technology, but his solution to it is a formula for solipsism or, as Keats charitably called it, the "Wordsworthian or egotistical sublime." Grandiosity ("The Poet binds together by passion and knowledge the vast empire of human society, as it is spread over the whole earth, and over all time") and isolation ("The Poet's own feelings are his stay and support") only feed and increase each other and, if their marriage is insular, only breed bombast. They infect the poet's soul and consequently his art, and can even become— as in the case of Delmore Schwartz and the dominant figures of Kunitz's generation—a risk to his life.

This danger is exactly what Whitman is addressing in this great passage from his preface to the 1855 edition of *Leaves of Grass:*

> The soul has that measureless pride which consists in never acknowledging any lessons but its own. But it has sympathy as measureless as its pride and the one balances the other and neither can stretch too far while it stretches in company with the other. The inmost secrets of art sleep with the twain.

The poet's "own feelings are his stay and support" for Whitman, too, but his "measureless pride"—essential to enduring the lack of an audience and its economic and psychological consequences—is offset by a "sympathy as measureless" for other people and even for other things outside of the self. This is the crucial counterweight to the egocentricity that is Whitman's explicit currency, and from the tension between them he makes his poetry: "The inmost secrets of art sleep with the twain." Tested by poverty and loneliness to the degree that he sometimes felt his poems "in a pecuniary and worldly sense have certainly wrecked the life of their author" (as Kunitz quotes him in his essay "At the Tomb of Walt Whitman"), the balance of measureless pride and sympathy is nonetheless the key to Whitman's spiritual discipline and probably to his survival.

It is also a remarkably accurate description of Stanley Kunitz. His poetry, his character, and his ideas are all born of these polarities. From his *Next to Last Things:*

If it were not for [the poet's] dream of perfection, which is the emblem of his life-enhancing art, and which he longs to share with others, generations of men and women would gradually sink into passivity, accepting as their lot second-rate or third-rate destinies, or worse. If one is to be taught submission, in the name of progress or national security, it is redemptive to recall the pride of one [Keats] who averred that his only humility was toward "the eternal Being, the Principle of Beauty, and the Memory of great Men."

The paradox, of course, is that a "life-enhancing art" which a poet "longs to share with others" isn't subject to the modification, opinion, or response of any other human being ("the eternal Being, the Principle of Beauty, and the Memory of great Men" being *ideas*), much less of any audience at large. And if the idea of the poet's preventing "generations" from sinking "into passivity" sounds very much like Wordsworth, in an earlier essay and different mood Kunitz shows himself to be aware of the hazards of such "measureless pride":

One of the dangers of poetry, certainly, is grandiosity. Let us not deceive ourselves: a poet isn't going to change the world with even the most powerful of his poems. The best he can hope for is to conquer a piece of himself.

In Kunitz's view, the spiritual discipline of poetry implies and incorporates the poet's social function. The poet is "an embodiment of resistance":

resistance against universal apathy, mediocrity, conformity, against institutional pressure to make everything look and become alike. This is why he is so involved with contraries.

He is "the representative man of our time":

The poet, in the experience of his art, is a whole person, or he is nothing. . . . He is uniquely equipped to defend the worth and power and responsibility of individuals in a world of institutions.

Consequently, and most pointedly:

The poet speaks to others not only through what he says but through what he is, his symbolic presence, as though he carried a set of flags reading Have a Heart, Let Nothing Get By, Live at the Center of Your Being. His life instructs us that it is not necessary, or even desirable, for everyone to join the crowds steaming onto the professional or business highway, pursuing the bitch goddess.

In other words (although a paraphrase is hardly needed), the poet's vocation has an important social function even if his poetry is drowned out by the noise of TV, movies, commercials, and factories spuming forth new products. It's a vocation inherently subversive to corporate ideology, spoken symbolically and by example:

Poets are subversive, but they are not really revolutionaries, for revolutionaries are concerned with changing others, while poets want first of all to change themselves.

If those dedicated to social change through civil disobedience spend a lot of time in jail, the poet's dedication to changing himself implies a life of internal exile in a society built for profit. Kunitz's most recent statement, in the *Paris Review* interview, is also his most urgent:

Evil has become a product of manufacture, it is built into our whole industrial and political system, it is being manufactured every day, it is rolling off the assembly lines, it is being sold in the stores, it pollutes the air. . . . Perhaps the way to cope with the adversary is to confront him in ourselves. We have to fight for our little bit of health. We have to make our living and dying important again. And the living and dying of others. Isn't that what poetry is about?

In this light, a poem as apparently apolitical as "My Sisters" takes on political content and becomes a political gesture, politically ineffective as it may be against mass-market movies and TV programs in which life is sentimentalized and death is trivialized. The political character of a poem has more to do with its rendering than with its subject, its ideas, or its rhetoric—by making us feel that living and dying are more important than property and "the national interest," and by using language clearly and accountably, unlike the way politicians and commercials use it. Insofar as the poet's vocation is a public act, it can be an act of conscience with a social function, even if the border between public and publicity in this media culture requires frequent monitoring. If the vocation of poetry Kunitz describes were arranged in a line, it would look like his characterization of "the power of the mind": "to transform," "to connect," and "to communicate"—the first ("to transform") being the poet's relation to himself through his spiritual discipline; the second ("to connect") his relation to the world and other people; and the third ("to communicate") his social role, through both his poetry and his "symbolic presence." Of course, it isn't a line. The poet's vocation is all these at once.

This outline of Kunitz's ideas really is "a kind of translation" from "the Arabian tongue" of his prose. He certainly never presents them this systematically. They have more vitality and nuance combined with his many other convictions, concerns, and affections. Reading his essays, I get a transfusion of his indomitable spirit, his "fierce hold on life," which is much more important to me than my agreement with his ideas. There are excellent reasons, for the sake of the poetry itself, to attempt to rescue its social function, even when from all appearances it surely has none. Poets from Horace to Sidney to Eliot have tried to do so, finding themselves at the edge of exile within the versions of civilization in which they lived. For Kunitz, poetry is a manifestation of hope and life, for the culture as well as for the individual. This is the source of its power and poignancy. He argues for the essential seriousness of poetry, and for clarity and depth and music at a time when otherwise intelligent critics, no doubt unconsciously reflecting the negligible social role of poetry, indulge triviality and praise the "originality" of superficial linguistic invention. He writes:

> In the best poetry of our time—but only the best—one is aware of a moral pressure being exerted on the medium in the very act of creation. By "moral" I mean a testing of existence at its highest pitch—what does it feel like to be totally oneself?; an awareness of

others beyond the self; a concern with values and meaning rather than with effects; an effort to tap the spontaneity that hides in the depths rather than what forms on the surface; a conviction about the possibility of making right and wrong choices. Lacking this pressure, we are left with nothing but a vacuum occupied by technique.

In exactly this sense, Kunitz's example to poets of my generation has been a moral example, put forward consciously with an awareness of the hazards of doing so. He has said, "The poet's first obligation is survival," by which he means spiritual as well as literal survival, knowing from experience the conflicts between the two for a poet in this culture: "No bolder challenge confronts the modern artist than to stay healthy in a sick world."

Visiting Stanley Kunitz years ago, during a difficult period, I made the standard complaints about the poet's life that anyone who has been around poets has heard a thousand times. That means he had heard them a hundred thousand times, and maybe even voiced them once or twice when he was living in absolute obscurity on almost no income, as he did for over twenty years before he won the Pulitzer Prize with a *Selected Poems* that was rejected by fourteen publishers. But he listened until I was finished, and then replied, "But, Michael, poetry is something you give to the world." If I'm ever able, as Chekhov said, "to squeeze the slave's blood out of my veins," this is the type of blood I'd replace it with.

A PHANTASMAGORIA

My Dream by Henry James

In my dream by Henry James there is a sentence:
"Stay and comfort your sea companion
for a while," spoken by an aging man
to a young one as they dawdle on the terrace
of a beachfront hotel. The young man doesn't know
how to feel—which is often the problem
in James, which may have been the problem
with James, living, as he said, *in* the work
("this is the only thing"), shaping his late
concerti of almost inaudible ephemerae
on the emotional scale. By 1980,
when this dream came to me, the line spoken
takes on sexual overtones, especially since
as the aging man says it he earnestly presses
the young man's forearm, and in James
no exchange between people is simple,
but the young man turns without answering
to gaze over the balustrade at the ocean,
over the pastel textures of beach umbrellas
and scalloped dresses whose hems brush the sand,
without guessing the aging man's loneliness
and desire for him. He sees only monotony

as he watches waves coming in, and this odd
old man who shared his parents' table on the ship
seems the merest disturbance of the air,
a mayfly at such distance he does not quite hear.
Why should I talk to anyone? glides over his mind
like a cloud above a pond
that mirrors what passes over and does not remember.
But I remember this cloud and this pond
from a midweek picnic with my mother
when I was still too little for school
and we were alone together
darkened by shadows of pines
when with both hands she turned my face
toward the cloud captured in the water
and everything I felt in the world was love for her.

In 1899, Henry James met Hendrik Andersen, his first love; eventually
they would vacation in Newport together. In 1900, at the age of fifty-
seven, James wrote to another young admirer:

> The port from which I set out was, I think, that of the essential
> loneliness of my life—and it seems to me the port, in sooth, to
> which again my course finally directs itself. This loneliness (since
> I mention it!)—what is it still but the deepest thing about one?
> Deeper about me, at any rate, than anything else, deeper than my
> "genius," deeper than my "discipline," deeper than my pride,
> deeper above all than the deep counter-minings of art.

The combination of this passage and the detail from James's biography is so obviously the starting point of my poem that readers may
find the fact interesting that it wasn't. When I had my dream and
drafted the poem, I neither had read this letter nor knew anything of
James's unhappy love affair with Andersen. The dream and the poem
were in fact the impetus to find out more about James's life, and I
didn't discover this information until much later, when the poem was
nearly finished. Of course the discovery flattened me. Even the dramatic setting of the dream is the terrace of a beachfront hotel, pre-

sumably in a port where the two characters recently landed. In his letter, James uses the word "port" figuratively, whereas the poem translates it into a literal place, as a dream might do with a remark heard during the day. And the subject of my poem is surely "essential loneliness," solitude and isolation (two very different things) set against the backdrop of a young child with his mother, a scene dug out of memory by the act of composition—in James's terms, one of the "deep counter-minings of art."

I've given up trying to explain the coincidences, although I guess I could have read James's letter somewhere years before and forgotten it. If so, it traveled some underground route through my psyche and acquired the texture and shape it takes in the poem. If this is what happened, the generation of this poem, strange as it would have been, would have been less strange than otherwise and would be more traceable than most poems of mine. They all arrive differently, indifferent to their origins, rarely fully grown, with their insistently individual set of character flaws and problems. Whatever useful and interesting things can be said about poetry, this part of it—its generation—seems a permanent mystery.

Yet there are great, persistent subjects. In *The Classical Tradition in Poetry*, Gilbert Murray says that for the Greeks they were "Love, Strife, Death, and that which is beyond Death." Loneliness, the port from which James says he set out, can touch all these both coming and going. It does in James's work, and I hope it does in my poem, because this is what gives the subject universality and dignity, as grief not a grievance. Otherwise, it is mere self-pity. Eliot's notion that "the emotion of art is impersonal" was no doubt a defensive one against the inevitable discomfort of self-exposure, but it was also a way to suggest that the emotion should be the poem's, not just the poet's. In fact, the emotion must eventually be the reader's, and the only way to do this is somehow to embody the emotion in the poem. How this happens is finally as mysterious and infinitely variable as the poem's generation, but it seems to have something to do with the poet's ability to regard the poem as a thing apart from him at the same time his personal commitment to it is most intense. In the poems I love by other poets, the emotion is so personal it seems to penetrate the superficial and not-so-superficial differences between us: the differences of gender, race, heritage, experience, and of wholly different eras and nations. How remarkable it really is to be touched by a twenty-four-year-old ex-surgeon's apprentice dead a hundred and seventy-five years, or by an Amherst lady of the 1860s "small, like the wren" with eyes "like the sherry in the glass, that the guest leaves," or by blind Homer, the anonymous bards of ancient Greece whose life and language must have been so unlike those of the United States now that in light of the one the other seems a dream. Or by the meticulous, impeccably toiletted, *fin-de-siècle* Henry James, whose background and temperament could not be more different from my own.

Anyway, for the sake of the "impersonal" and however it came about, I was happy to be given the *donnée* of my poem. Once in 1980, I did awake with the sentence "Stay and comfort your sea companion for a while," spoken by an aging man to a young one, from a dream which—what can I say?—was authored by Henry James. Looking back now, I can see how the whole poem issues from that beginning, although these lines sat on, in, under, and away from my desk for about a year or so before they yielded much more of the poem. I only know how to work one way, from the first syllable to the last; as I get older I seem to be able to allow some of the syllables to temporarily satisfy me less in the belief that they may have an important role in the whole shape and in the hope that they will be changed into something better later on. The beginning of "My Dream by Henry James" gave me the characters and got the story going but, more importantly, made a window I would eventually see the rest of the poem through in language I found compelling. This of course is the main thing: what the language says is only part of what it is, and probably not the best part. I liked the sound, rhythm, and syntax of these lines—the rhymes, half-rhymes, and assonances such as "a while, dawdle, hotel" and "companion, aging man, young one" and "sentence, terrace." In free verse, the grammatical unit of the sentence usually dominates the rhythmical unit of the line, because the line doesn't adopt the identifying characteristics of end-rhyme or uniform meter. But free verse allows at least as great a richness of formal interaction of the words, and may therefore allow a different but no less complete instrumentality of the language. The greatest pleasure for me in writing poetry occurs when the form language acquires in arrangement vies for my attention with the meaning of the words, when the two in conjunction seem to be shaping each other. This is a bodily pleasure. It's a wonderful feeling when the form of a poem, the pattern of the words-in-arrangement, seems to be telling you what the poem itself wants to be.

In the fall of 1980, about nine months after I first drafted "My Dream by Henry James," an Edward Hopper exhibit opened at the Whitney Museum. I was living in Princeton, New Jersey, and kept taking the train into New York to see it, and couldn't have said why much more exactly than could an animal that's drawn to a particular place. I loved the paintings, but there was something more in them I was looking for. They seemed both abstract and representational, that if you switched something in your brain a millionth of a degree you could see the picture of a tunnel or of the couple on the front porch in summer as a pure shape. I remember when I finally saw the paintings both ways at once: the form and the thing represented seemed to merge while simultaneously remaining distinct, and the tension between them became almost tangible. It was a *physical* sensation. I stopped in front of the painting I was looking at—it was *Approaching a City*—and prayed that somehow I would be able to do this in my poetry.

I worked on "My Dream by Henry James" off and on for the next year. I wrote it again and again from the beginning but couldn't finish it. Literally finish it. I couldn't find the right ending, although I tried an embarrassingly wide selection. Then I tried to frame it differently. At one stage, the speaker became a critic who fell asleep in his office (bad idea); in another version, the young man's death in the First World War was foreshadowed (very bad idea). As I often do when all else fails, I began criticizing the poem in the margins before putting it away. "Use the language to direct," one draft says in block print, and "This is a thorough setting and what the poem now needs is that move, or turn, inside." I was stuck in the dramatic situation of the dream, at the line "a mayfly at such distance he does not quite hear." I knew the poem had to go beyond or beneath the dream somehow, and had to do so with a kind of turn, or *volta,* the way a sonnet turns between the octave and sestet. All I had was an abstract sense of the shape and movement.

Is this why the scene that finally seemed right to me involves an image of arrested movement, of arrested time? And turns inside, into the speaker's memory, to the remembrance itself, and, further, into his feelings at that moment of childhood? I don't have answers to these questions. The poem tries to move through layers of association in a speaking voice that's capable of ornate criticisms in Jamesian diction ("shaping his late / concerti of almost inaudible ephemerae") and even quotes James's notebooks ("'this is the only thing'"). But at the end something essential seemed called for, beneath elaborations and estrangements. If the poem does issue from its first sentence, I hope the last sentence absorbs and transmutes all that preceded it, denying none of the "essential loneliness" but shaping it.

"There is always a phantasmagoria," said Yeats, and the word implies a rapidity of movement that seems to me essential to poetry. And when the poet is "most himself," Yeats continues, "he is never the bundle of accidence and incoherence that sits down to breakfast." If "My Dream by Henry James" works, whatever it has to do with me personally is probably the least interesting thing about it. Every poem has to be credible, and for most readers now this means they have to believe someone is speaking to them. Maybe at an extreme moment of my dream-life I was inhabited by the ghost of Henry James. I would like to think so. The poem is surely critical of him—to live *in* the work instead of in the world, I firmly believe, will eventually eviscerate the work. But this notion has many subtle complications, and it was also part of my intention in writing the poem to pay homage to James's many, many beautiful sentences.

CONSIDER A MOVE

Consider a Move

The steady time of being unknown,
in solitude, without friends,
is not a steadiness that sustains.
I hear your voice waver on the phone:

Haven't talked to anyone for days.
I drive around, I sit in parking lots.
The voice zeroes through my ear, and waits.
What should I say? There are ways

to meet people you will want to love?
I know of none. You come out stronger
having gone through this? I no longer
believe that, if I once did. Consider a move,

a change, a job, a new place to live,
some place you'd like to be. *That's not it,*
you say. Now time curves back. We almost touch.
Then what is? I ask. What is?

I wrote "Consider a Move" almost twenty-five years ago. I remember
very well the phone conversation it portrays. What may not be evident
is the exact nature of the relationship between the two characters.
That's for the reader to fill in. The poem chooses not to include nar-

rative information in order not to distract from the dramatic focus on the speaker's internal conflict, his attempt to resolve the conflict between his sympathy and his frustration with the person in crisis and also the difference in his own feelings for that person between the present moment of the conversation and the lost moments of the past.

It was the first poem I had ever written in a fixed form. Like most young poets in the seventies and since, I grew up reading and writing free verse. When I was a student at Iowa from 1970 to 1974, nobody was writing in rhyme and meter, including me, so I made a study of prosody, reading a great many stultifying treatises starting with Saintsbury's, and tried to teach myself how to do it. There were many poems I loved that could not exist outside of a fixed form—imagine Hardy's "The Self Unseeing" without the trimeter quatrains—and I wanted to be able to write poems like these if they came to me. The problem was to find a way to make the form flexible, to use it instead of being impeded by it, while keeping the voice credible and rooted in the rhythms of speech. I wanted the fixed form to be generative, and I wasn't about to transpose word order for the sake of filling out a rhyme or metrical grid (the last thing I wanted was for any of my poems to sound stilted or old-fashioned).

I am still happy with "Consider a Move" as a technical exercise. Readers have told me that they have read it many times before realizing it was in envelope quatrains, and this pleases me inordinately. Since there are no objects in the poem except the phone, and the poem consists entirely of the speaker's thoughts and the represented dialogue, the quatrains serve to lend palpability and organization to those most impalpable and disorganized things: thought and speech. Frost said that he liked to see the way a sentence lay across a stanza, and I hope he might like the way these do here: the composition of the sentences in relationship to the line, and the line in relationship to the sentences, and the pattern of them from stanza to stanza, including the resolution. In the best poems, this feels as happy as music, despite any unhappiness portrayed. When a traditional form seems solidly fixed but lightly used, it can provide at least a modest instance of what Yeats meant by "gaiety transfiguring all that dread," which I understand to mean the gaiety of making.

INFLUENCE AND MASTERY

Reminder

Torment by appetite
is itself an appetite
dulled by inarticulate,
dogged, daily

loving-others-to-death—
as Chekhov put it, "compassion
down to your fingertips"—,
looking on them as into the sun

not in the least for their sake
but slowly for your own
because it causes
the blinded soul to bloom

like deliciousness in dirt,
like beauty from hurt,
their light—*their* light—
pulls so surely. Let it.

"Reminder" was sparked by a conversation with my friend, Jim McMichael, about Emmanuel Levinas's notion of the "alterity of the Other" that is both "the alterity of the human Other and of the Most-High." For Levinas, "the intelligibility of transcendence lies outside ontological structures" and "bears an ethical sense or direction." His argument is that "the structure of transcendence is exemplified not by religious experience" in solitude but by "the ethical," behavior toward other people. Although Levinas was a Lithuanian Jew, his idea seemed to me a radical, illuminating re-vision of the traditional Christian notion that faith without good works is dead: for Levinas, it is possible to experience God only in action toward others. Simone Weil said almost the same thing when she wrote that if you give a crust to a beggar in the right spirit it will save *your* soul (emphasis hers). Levinas, a Holocaust survivor, added, "And you must take the bread from your own mouth."

Emily Dickinson practiced her own version of this "compassion down to your fingertips" and often wrote about it:

> The Service without Hope -
> Is tenderest, I think -
> Because 'tis unsustained
> By stint - Rewarded Work -
>
> Has impetus of Gain -
> And impetus of Goal -
> There is no Diligence like that
> That knows not an Until -
>
>   #880F [779] (1864)*

When I wrote "Reminder," I was about four years into a still-unfinished sequence of sixteen-line poems in quatrains and an immersion in Dickinson's work that also continues. She has certainly "influenced" me, a word whose Latin root means the flowing of an ethereal fluid or power from the stars, thought by Roman astrologers

---

* The texts and numbers of Emily Dickinson's poems are from *The Complete Poems of Emily Dickinson: Variorum Edition,* edited by R. W. Franklin (Harvard University Press, 1998). The numbers in brackets are from *The Complete Poems of Emily Dickinson,* edited by Thomas H. Johnson (Little Brown and Co., 1960)—the standard edition of her work until superseded by Franklin's .

to affect a person's character and actions. Dickinson knew herself to be a person who could be this powerfully influenced by writing, and indeed was this powerfully influenced, by the Bible and Shakespeare, and lesser constellations. That she knew she could be even more powerfully influenced by people is evident from her first letters and poems, and is part of the reason behind her famous withdrawal from society at large into a society of intimates, a cloister that has been disfiguringly popularized as neurotic isolation and even agoraphobia.

"Reminder," as I hope is clear, is addressed to myself. The last sentence of the poem ("Let it") is meant to occur in a continuous present, the moment in the poem merged with the moment of reading it. As Dickinson said, "Forever is composed of nows." This intense focus she had I constantly forget. I need many reminders, and this poem is one of them. All of my sixteen-line poems in quatrains, including this one, have been influenced (and inspired) by Dickinson's remarkably various and rich adaptations of the hymn stanza. Some of this range can be seen in the three poems I want to discuss in this essay (see pp. 136–37). She uses the stanza as a structural grid with slant rhymes at the joists, a recurring melody against the rhythmical and grammatical counterpoint of her sentences, which themselves are often counterpointed against conventional grammar through the agency of the dashes. It is an inimitable poetic style, technically brilliant. My ambition in "Reminder" and the other poems in my sequence is much more modest: simply to use the form differently each time and make sure the particular usage is grounded in the particular poem's structure and subject. She accomplished this over and over again in her 1789 poems and thirty years of writing. For her to have done so, it must have been part of her intention, yet how she learned such intentions, much less such mastery in realizing them, is a mystery.

Another aspect of her mysterious mastery is somewhat more traceable. Despite their variety, what these three poems of hers have in common is what Jay Leyda in his introduction to his documentation of Dickinson's "Years and Hours" mistakenly called the "omitted center": "The riddle, the circumstance too well known to be repeated to the initiate, the deliberate skirting of the obvious—this was the means she used to increase the privacy of her communication." On the contrary, it is by omitting anecdote and incident that she arrives at the "center" in these poems, the place of public communication where the poem is about the reader not the writer, where language articulates not merely the writer's temporary feelings but permanent human feeling and thereby transfigures her private feelings, contextualizes them, and illuminates them. This, as Dickinson well knew, is a religious experience, analogous to using the New Testament's story of Christ to transfigure, contextualize, and illuminate similar moments in any person's life. But she accomplishes it through rhetoric not narrative, by writing a poem not preaching the Gospel, by the authority of human words not God's. All three poems are arguments. She doesn't tell us what occasioned her blessing (767 [#756]) or pain (515 [#599]) or shame (1349 [#1304]), but deals in their effects. There is no information in the poem that separates her from us. The poem is made to be an experience instead of referring to one, which is precisely how she says she knows poetry in her famous remark to Higginson: "If I read a book [and] it makes my whole body so cold no fire ever can warm me I know *that* is poetry. If I feel physically as if the top of my head were taken off, I know *that* is poetry. These are the only way I know it. Is there any other way."

I am trying to learn how she learned to write like this. Rhetoric was one of her main subjects during her year at Mount Holyoke Seminary. Her text there was Samuel P. Newman's *A Practical System of Rhetoric.* It is still an interesting and sophisticated book, astonishingly so for high-school students (impossibly so for today's high-school students). Newman writes, "The first and leading object of attention in every composition of an argumentative kind, is to determine the precise point of inquiry—the proposition which is to be laid down and supported." All three poems have such a proposition, but the ways they are "laid down and supported" differ wildly and wonderfully, and constitute a short lesson in the depth of her skill. "One Blessing had I than the rest" is the simplest: proposition (stanza 1), evidence (stanzas 2–4), conclusion (stanza 5). Its conventional argumentative structure, dull in the hands of Dickinson's Victorian contemporaries, here grounds a subject, mind, and linguistic inventiveness alive in every line. The solidity of structure, and its coincidence with stanza form, allows for point-to-point variation and improvisation. "There is a pain - so utter -" works differently. The proposition stated in the first two lines is then integrated into a personified drama that is also a description of human response to utter pain—neither a particular human nor a particular pain, much less her or hers, whatever utter pain may have sparked her writing it. The argument is implicit and enacted, and a second drama ("as one within a swoon") is generated from the first by the pivotal simile, which always implies the mind of the speaker. Her mind is active throughout. We experience her rein- terpreting her own words when "swallows" changes from metaphor to dramatic action at the moment the utter pain *"covers* the Abyss with Trance -". The compounding of the initial action makes us focus on what such utter pain *does,* and what it does, in the last six lines of the poem, is surprisingly palliative, as if such pain contains its own act of grace that allows the sufferer to survive. And what a sentence the poem is—as complex and clear as a sentence can be, laid across eight lines, counterpointed by the famous dashes that in her manu- script of this poem are uniform but often are more like dots or like diagonals slashed up or down.

That's how they are in the manuscript of "Not with a Club, the Heart is broken"—which is impossible to reproduce typographically. The poem is lined like this:

Not with a
Club, the Heart
is broken
Nor with a
Stone
A Whip so
small you
could not see it
I've known

To lash the
Magic Creature
till it fell,
Yet that Whip's

Name
too noble then
to tell.

Magnanimous
as Bird
By Boy descried-
Singing unto the
Stone
of which it died-

Shame need not
    crouch
In such an Earth
as Our's.
Shame—Stand Erect.
The Universe is your's.

This manuscript, unlike the two earlier ones from the fascicles, looks strikingly private—the stanzas are on the page but the lines are only in her ear. The argument, too, is more unruly than those of either earlier poem. The proposition takes two stanzas to state in its entirety, and is composed of three smaller propositions: (1) the Heart (conventional symbol for the seat of feeling) is not broken by weapons that break the body; (2) the Heart (characterized as "the Magic Creature") is broken by something invisible (characterized as "A Whip"); (3) the name of that whip (or the person wielding it) may not be revealed because it is "too noble" to the person testifying or at least to this person giving this testimony or perhaps to society at large. The three smaller propositions go from public (even commonplace) to invisible to secret. Nor is that secret revealed by the rest of the poem. If the argument moves forward, it does so obliquely. The third stanza is an unattached sentence fragment, a comparison made by the speaker about the speaker or about anyone in the speaker's position—less evidence than testimony dramatized through figures. (Dickinson often uses birds to stand for herself.) The first sentence of the last stanza is the conclusion: "Shame need not crouch in such an earth as ours"—shame (personified) need not be invisible or secret. But the conclusion begins another argument, in the surprising form of a command, a direct address to Shame, the sort of oblique movement that occurred in the break between stanza two and three but is here contained within a stanza. The reason Shame need not be invisible is that it owns the universe. The speaker's anguish and fury in this moment of the poem are amplified by the direct address, which enacts dramatically the speaker's attempt to distinguish Shame from herself while paradoxically asserting its universal dominance.

Dickinson's mastery here is manifold, and the insight behind it is based on a profound acquaintance with how shame pervades identity and destroys it, which brings us back from cosmos to microcosm, the Heart's being lashed until "it fell." The argument as a whole is at best circular, but as Higginson wrote in *Atlantic Essays* (which Dickinson read both as the individual essays appeared in the *Atlantic Monthly* and as a book when it was published in 1871), "In what is called poetry, *belles-lettres,* or pure literature, the osseous structure is of course hidden; and the symmetry suggested is always that of taste rather than of logic, though logic must always be implied, or at least never violated." "Taste" was one of the main critical terms of the day, and does indeed suggest the symmetry of "Not with a Club, the Heart is broken." According to Newman, "As the result of past experiences of emotions, certain principles seem fixed in the mind, and when taste is called into exercise, it is the immediate application of these principles to particular instances." Poems may have arguments, but they also have many other generative tools and triggers, from large musical patterns to syntactical and sonic rhythms to "past experiences of emotions."

When such compelling poems as this one walk the edge of unintelligibility, it is natural to try to make them more accessible by looking for hints in the person behind the act of speech (or writing) that characterizes her. We want to know exactly what her "past experiences of emotions" were. This is probably why Dickinson has been the subject of rampant biographical speculation ever since the first edition of her poems (which so many readers immediately found "strange" and "powerful") appeared in 1890, four years after her death. The surviving biographical evidence around "Not with a Club" is tantalizing, as usual. Dickinson made a copy of the poem on a sheet which Ralph Franklin describes as "wove, cream, and blue-ruled; the stationery is embossed CONGRESS above a capitol." Franklin dates it "about 1873– 74" in the manuscript holographs and 1874 in the *Variorum Edition*. Dickinson's father died in 1874. A former United States Congressman, he was serving in the state legislature in Boston, gave a speech on the house floor, felt weak afterwards, walked back to his rented room to which a physician was summoned who apparently gave him opium he was allergic to, and he died. Why would Emily Dickinson copy a poem about shame on her father's official stationery? Maybe for no reason at all, since she seemed to have used any and all available scraps of paper. On the same set of two sheets is "The way to know the Bobolink," which is one of her many poems about how to see the natural world à la Emerson and Blake through the eye, not with it, but does also contain these "lines":

He compliments
Existence
Until allured
Away

By Seasons
  or his Children
Adult and
urgent grown-

Between the two poems is an *x* and the word "possibly" above a two-inch horizontal line (probably the marks of her first editor, Millicent Todd Bingham), below which is the first stanza of "Not with a Club." Did she write these two poems after her father died? When did she copy them onto his stationery? What do they have to do with him?

The other tantalizing bit surrounding a poem about the absolute power of shame is the article that Emily Dickinson certainly read in *The Springfield Republican* on September 24, 1874. It was written by Judge Otis Phillip Lord and it was about the greatest scandal of the day: the revelation of the longtime extramarital affair between Elizabeth Tilton and Henry Ward Beecher, the famous minister and abolitionist. The Beechers were longtime family friends of the Dickinsons, and Emily Dickinson was in love with Judge Lord, who was her father's age. Whether or not she was in love with him in 1874, while his wife was still alive, is unknown, but she (later?) owned a ring with his middle name engraved inside the band, and her sister Vinnie's last gesture over her coffin was to put two heliotropes by her hand "to take to Judge Lord," who had died two years before. His article in *The Springfield Republican* concluded that Beecher was guilty of adultery.

However "Not with a Club" came to be written, whatever personal shame Emily Dickinson suffered or observed, the poem is ours now. It was also ours when she wrote it, because of the way she wrote. Her mastery derives from a dedication to truth and a belief in her lexicon: the power of language-in-poetry to present truth. This, I think, is what she meant by "my business is circumference" (a term she must have first encountered in reading Emerson): the circle of human articulation is widened, the terra incognita within the circle becomes known. It is mapped by the poem in the writing, forever there for us to discover in reading it—provided that we learn how to read it, which continues to be the challenge of Dickinson's poems, since they continue to be almost as unconventional as they were when she wrote them. Her mastery of grammar and rhetoric were so complete that her failed experiments with them constitute a failure of English to do what she asks of it, although it answered her more often than it didn't. At her best, she put the greatest pressure on it, with faith in its ability to bear it—a direct analogy to her relationship to God. Her love of other people was generous and complex and (as it is for the rest of us) specific in character to the person she loved, and sometimes it was so intense as to constitute what she called "idolatry." "I do not respect 'doctrines,'" she said (quoting the word to emphasize her disdain)— "doctrines" of orthodox grammar no less than of orthodox religion, but in both cases she seems to have absorbed everything in them that was useful to her. Her humility is in her understanding that language like God was here before she was, but she used all of her intelligence, wit, courage, and talent to leave them both changed. In my opinion, she did.

One Blessing had I than the rest
So larger to my Eyes
That I stopped gauging - satisfied -
For this enchanted size -

It was the limit of my Dream -
The focus of my Prayer -
A perfect - paralyzing Bliss -
Contented as Despair -

I knew no more of Want - or Cold -
Phantasms both become
For this new Value in the Soul -
Supremest Earthly Sum -

The Heaven below the Heaven above -
Obscured with ruddier Blue -
Life's Latitudes leant over - full -
The Judgement perished - too -

Why Bliss so scantily disburse -
Why Paradise defer -
Why Floods be served to Us - in Bowls -
I speculate no more -

                    767 [#756] (1863)

There is a pain - so utter -
It swallows substance up -
Then covers the Abyss with Trance -
So Memory can step
Around - across - upon it -
As one within a Swoon -
Goes safely - where an open eye -
Would drop Him - Bone by Bone.
                    515 [#599] (1863)

Not with a Club, the Heart is broken
Nor with a Stone -

A Whip so small you could not see it
I've known

To lash the Magic Creature
Till it fell,
Yet that Whip's Name
Too noble then to tell.

Magnanimous as Bird
By Boy descried -
Singing unto the Stone
Of which it died -

Shame need not crouch
In such an Earth as Our's -
Shame - stand erect -
The Universe is your's.

                    1349 [1304] (1874)

TELL ME A STORY

When I was little boy, my father told me bedtime stories about the Greenies. The Greenies were a race of tiny people—three feet tall—who lived inside the earth. My father had discovered them when he was my age exploring caves in the Ozarks where he grew up on a dirt farm. He'd entertain himself climbing deep down in the dark, among bats and stalagmites and stalactites, further down than anyone had ever gone. One day, he saw an odd light coming through a crack above a ledge high up in the cave wall, almost hidden by rocks. He climbed up and by moving the rocks he saw an opening just large enough for him to squeeze through. There was a ledge on the other side, too, and there in the great cavern beneath him, in a shining city made of emeralds, diamonds, platinum, and gold, he saw the Greenies, all scurrying this way and that like ants. It was terrifically hot and damp, the stones around him radiated heat. When he climbed down closer he could see their pale-green skin tough as rhinoceros hide and their corkscrew-tipped heads that could drill through granite. There was a good Greenie king, a gorgeous Greenie princess who was in love with my father (gorgeous, I guess, despite her corkscrew-tipped head), bad Greenies who had left the city and threatened it with raids, and assorted natural cataclysms and fantastic monsters.

The detail I remember best was incidental to the big battles and epic struggle for racial survival. After my father had helped the Greenies and been accepted and honored by them, he was given full access to their kingdom, permission never before granted to an outsider. He

138

could roam about wherever he wanted and treat whatever they had as his own—the latter privilege he didn't exercise except for the three modest, perfect diamonds he took for his mother, for the woman he would someday marry (this diamond could be found in my mother's engagement ring), and for himself (here was his, in the gold ring on his right hand; he said someday, when he was dead, it would be mine). One quiet day in the kingdom, happy and content with these harmonious, gentle people, he was exploring its outer reaches by himself and, in a grotto on the other side of a stream, he came upon a goat with a head exactly like the lampshade on the floor lamp next to my bed—narrow at the top and opening out—and, behind the goat, emerging from the shadows, the most beautiful woman he had ever seen, completely naked. Then the grotto began pulsing with a strange light. They stared at him, woman and goat. He knew if he crossed the stream his life would be changed. He'd never see his parents again, or maybe even the Greenies. The woman smiled invitingly but the goat hissed and out of its lampshade skull came poison smoke. My father turned and ran, on to the next wonder and adventure. Although I'm sure I asked about them, they never appeared in the stories again.

After that I couldn't look at the lamp without seeing the goat. It had two simultaneous beings. In the daylight, it was the lamp *and* the goat, or the goat functioning as a lamp, and at night when the light was turned out it became the goat, perfectly still, an immobile outline permanently suspended in the instant before it would start to move and spume poison smoke. It sent a chill through me from toes to scalp, an awful thrill that was finally too much, and made me feel like I was spinning wildly in outer space. But when my father was sitting on the edge of the bed with his elbows on his knees, I could see his white shirt in the dark, I could feel the pressure of his hips, and that contact grounded me enough so that no matter how scared or crazy I became I wanted him to keep telling me the stories.

He didn't tell them often—each time had to be a special treat. And each time, before he would begin, he'd ask me if I believed in the Greenies. I had to say yes to get a story, to say I believed that this fabulous world was going on inside the earth even as he spoke. I didn't believe it, then I said I did, and as the word left my mouth I believed and didn't believe at the same time—like the goat-lamp. It was secret life. It was my father's secret life. He had made it from the basic stuff of the Old Testament, Buck Rogers, and H. Rider Haggard (*King Solomon's Mines*)—his favorite author—but also from his own childhood memories, probably some of the fondest he had, of being brave and adventurous, exploring caves by himself. Although he was the storyteller in our family, he almost never told me anything about *his* father, who was an alcoholic (like himself). His father's absence from his stories only now seems significant to me. The stories were cautionary and instructional, exemplifying courage I was meant to emulate, invariably dramatizing his lonely battle with the world. He was always alone in them. Clearly, that was his memory of himself—or, more accurately, my memory of his memory of himself, communicated to me most powerfully in the Greenie stories (hybrids of memory and fantasy that they were): the hero against a hostile world. My dad was the hero. I absorbed the message like a soft little sponge, the way only a child can. I wanted to be like my dad. I wanted to be the hero, too.

But why tell this story of these stories? In a remarkable essay about his father in his almost-forgotten book of autobiographical essays, *Court of Memory,* James McConkey writes, "Memory, which gives us our identities, can, by an act of grace, release us from ourselves to an outpouring of its most hidden contents." My father's stories—his memory and identity—wounded me almost too deeply for words but also gave me life. They are engraved in me. Stories are the way we articulate ourselves to ourselves, as well as to one another. We tell hundreds of stories every day. Through their agency we make the amorphous, inexhaustible inner into the shapely, provisional outer. They are an irreplaceable way of knowing and mode of social intercourse (notwithstanding our dominant "efficient" scientific models of knowledge and social organization). Their material is the material of memory, which is generative, not a passive lump of stuff. One does not take a memory and make it into a story. Memory itself makes the story—and, as McConkey implies, we can be released not only *by* its story but also *to* it. Memory is both the subject and predicate of which we are the objects.

In this regard, the only difference between fiction and nonfiction is how faithful the writer must be to memory and how willing he is to rein it in when it gallops toward fantasy, for which it's also the source. Surely writing fiction—and reading it—can also produce that graceful release McConkey is talking about. Every reader of this essay has experienced the rapture of reading a piece of writing that *takes* you, an experience of art that probably reproduces an experience in life—of being "flooded" by memory, of tapping into an underground stream that seems simply to burst forth. But memory is always there, implicitly telling us what to feel and think, what we like and don't, who we are. "Memory . . . gives us our identities": we don't have memory: it has us—as if it were a container and an engine in which we are also contained, by which we are driven. How deeply we are formed by what happens to us, who we're born to, the previous generations who live in us. We are probably also what happened to them, even if we don't know what that is or even who they were, shards embedded in stories and chromosomes. No wonder we are such mysteries to ourselves. Our feelings are grounded in sources that will elude us no matter what reductive psychoanalytic explanations we construct to manage them or how many ingenious drugs are designed to alter them. "The eye sees what it has been given to see by concrete circumstances," wrote Flannery O'Connor, "and the imagination reproduces what, by some related gift, it is able to make live." How that moment of seeing the goat-lamp shaped me exceeds my powers of analysis but, in O'Connor's terms, maybe not the power of imagination—by becoming part of a story.

The discipline of writing includes a special opportunity for the writer as a person to make an interpersonal object that not only expresses his feelings but also embodies them, that makes them both accessible to him and strangely independent of him. This is writing's gift to the writer and, like all large gifts, it carries a large obligation. O'Connor again:

> In the act of writing, one sees that the way a thing is made controls and is inseparable from the whole meaning of it. The form of a story gives it meaning which any other form would change.

It's precisely this that distinguishes rendering from remembering—
or reporting, which is merely remembering with a pen in your hand
(a tape recorder, in the case of the celebrity memoir). To use Henry
James's favorite term for it, the writer has to "do" the thing he writes
about. Through this "doing," the writer's unfathomable, private feelings are transformed into apprehensible, shared language. Such a
complete transformation could happen in talk if talk weren't ephem-
eral, local, and unrevisable, if what was discovered in talk were
worked over and made palpable (the way James worked over dinner-
party conversation *données* into novels). It's this lack of writing's discipline applied to subjects that require the utmost discipline that
makes bad memoirs so bad and afternoon talk shows so embarrassing—not, as some newspaper book critics have asserted, the subjects
themselves. Shame becomes a circus act on Jenny Jones, but in the
hands of a writer like Kafka (or O'Connor, or James, or Chekhov, or
Shakespeare—the list could be extended to every great writer we
have) it is an essential and inexhaustible subject, given a shape we can
understand and deeply need to understand. It becomes social, public,
part of shared culture, and thereby takes on significance. Whereas,
left to fester and gnaw one isolated psyche, shame is only murderous.
Did Kafka save his life by writing? Maybe not, but he has helped to
save others. Mine, for one.

The most surprising personal aspect of writing my autobiography
was discovering the emotional weight of events I had thought not so
important to me. Because they were important to the story, they demonstrated how important they were to me. People I knew only briefly
affected me more than I had ever guessed. It was as if the story itself
called them up from the depths and showed me how to see them.
Some of them I had almost forgotten, submerged in that underground stream of memory that the daily concentration of writing
tapped into. My narrative—"the telling of events in time"—formed
itself from the events memory had to tell.

But I also shaped the narrative, and, in this regard, I was continuously interacting with memory. By reading what I wrote, I perceived certain subjects—shame (and its compulsive sexual expression) prominent among them; growing up male, Catholic, and white

in America; the hellish economic pressure on a middle-class family; a boy's love/hate of his alcoholic father—and these subjects became the book's subject much more than what happened to me, which matters only as illustration, one instance of how these subjects impinged on one of many individual and unrepeatable lives: a testimony not a confession. The subjects became a principle of selection from the mass of all that happened to me, all the people I knew, all that was said or thought; and this principle, if I may call it that, pushed and pulled against incidents and characters that insisted on being part of the story. As Nabokov put it, "The following of thematic designs through one's life should be the true purpose of autobiography." This requires the exercise of the autobiographer's critical faculties, and the more talented a critic he is of his own life the better his book is likely to be—a talent he must exercise more explicitly than the novelist, and more certainly, since his misconceptions will be everywhere evident. In O'Connor's words,

> The writer has to judge himself with a stranger's eye and a stranger's severity. . . . No art is sunk in the self, but rather, in art the self becomes self-forgetful in order to meet the demands of the thing seen and the thing being made.

But is this really possible when the writer's own life is the subject? Can autobiography ever be "self-forgetful," as O'Connor rightly asserts art must be? It can only if the life of the story is the main thing— the life of the story, paradoxically, *not* the life of the autobiographer, which is merely the raw material of the story. The autobiographer must be mindful of the prerogatives and imperatives of the story in every way a novelist must be, and must be equally faithful to it, and no less able than a novelist to enter the points of view of the characters at their specific times and places, especially his own. My task was not only to make the reader feel how it felt to be me; it was to make me feel how it felt to be me. In the act of writing, I relived the experience I was writing about—and I also didn't, because it was also becoming language, with the frustration and exhilaration which always accompanies that. When I lived those experiences as a child and teenager and young man there was plenty of frustration and precious little exhilaration, and none of it of the writerly kind. I felt lost and indeed was lost, never for a moment imagining that it all would someday become "material." Now the conditions of my life had changed. I was an adult (finally), no longer literally at the mercy of the conditions I was dramatizing. The writing helped me to be no longer at the mercy of these conditions emotionally, either—the release McConkey calls an act of grace. I needed the task of rendering my life, a contract with the reader which obliged me to honor the facts. I knew the gift of the story was wrapped in what actually happened (as memory remembered it and writing might render it)—the gift of the story to me and, I hoped, to the reader. "The reader" was oddly and exclusively *in* the act of writing itself. I wrote to the book, to the story, not to any person, real, imagined, or hypostatized. The aesthetic and ethical relationships between me and this reader-in-the-writing were identical: getting it down right was right.

Needless to say, however, this put me in conflict with myself— between me as a writer and as a person—over the revelations the story contained, that this story had to contain in order to be told. There was no avoiding them. As William Maxwell said in an interview:

> Sometimes I have suffered the torments of the damned in describing real people, where I was sure that I was, perhaps, causing pain. And in this struggle the artist won out. There was a point at which I would not give up something that I knew was right. Aesthetically. And artistically.

And he was talking about fiction, with its built-in ethical safety valve. No reader confuses Ishmael with Melville, or Nick Carraway with F. Scott Fitzgerald, or the unhappy husband who narrates "The Kreutzer Sonata" with Tolstoy (except the U.S. Post Office Department, which wouldn't deliver the American newspapers that serialized it, and Senator Theodore Roosevelt, who denounced its author as a "sexual moral pervert"). But the narrator of an autobiography, in the reader's mind, *is* the author—the person, in the flesh, who pays his taxes and shops for bagels.

This identification for the writer is both aesthetically and ethically perilous. "How could this guy publish this about his wife?" is not a question that occurs these days to most readers of "The Kreutzer Sonata." But such questions naturally do occur to readers of autobiographies, and they are much muddled at present in this atmosphere of promiscuous exposure à la Jenny Jones and the shame circus, and the deadbolt linkage of information and promotion that pervades our media-culture, in which what people are saying seems invariably connected to something they're selling (*vide* the Author Book Tour, apparently pioneered in our era by—who else?—Jacqueline Susann). Why should autobiographers be expected to be disinterested when nobody else seems to be? Much less about the representation of one's self and one's life, with its potential effects on one's well-being? Why should we not read autobiographies, especially ones that deal with intimate subjects and personal revelations, as mere "tell-alls," "domestic confessionals," and "autopathographies" (to cite just three hostile journalistic coinages): an inherently repugnant form of narcissistic merchandising, self-display, and self-promotion?

The book itself has to answer such questions—formally, in *its* character and tone—not the writer, on talk shows or anywhere else. If the writer's privacy is sacrificed for the book's intimacy, it may be worth it if the book is worth it, although that will not relieve "the torments of the damned" he may suffer, since how can he ever be sure his book is worth it? How can he compare his family's feelings to the good his book does and is? Books and people are not comparable. But the terms of art and life are deeply entangled, as they are in the writer himself as an artist and a human being. In my experience, there are no formulas to answer the ethical questions that arise when publishing an autobiography, except to ask for the permission of the people whose lives are exposed by it, much less the questions that arise while writing it, at moments when the ethical wages unconditional war on the aesthetic. If that weren't enough to contend with, the autobiographer's failure to win the reader's suspension of disbelief is probably even more deadly than the novelist's. He is condemned to tell his story in the first person, which complicates his problems no end. Just getting off center stage so the story can speak is a daunting technical and temperamental challenge that demands, among other things, preternatural psychological tact. Self-consciousness is as fatal as the lack of it, especially in the intricate business of self-portrayal. An excessively proprietary interest in his main character (himself) will sink his story like a pair of concrete boots. An autobiographer who does not constantly torment himself with the question "Is this interesting to anyone else?" is probably going to write a book that isn't. Without invention, he must fascinate us as much as a novelist with the endlessly interesting interactions between character (people) and plot (what happens to them), just as we are fascinated in and by our own lives.

Yet autobiography can achieve a quality of intimacy that does distinguish the experience of reading it (and writing it). How intimate should a story be? As intimate as it has to be, is the only answer I know. Each age has its idea of decorum, although we have come to expect art to violate it, so that the violation is sometimes now mistaken for the art and romanticized as "transgression," as if social and aesthetic conventions were identical and bad manners equaled artistic innovation. On the opposing side, the genteel tradition of criticism has always confused the beautiful and the agreeable, and the value of privacy with the conventions of secrecy. Maybe because most of my childhood reading was done in bed, alone in the halo of a small overhead lamp that seemed to define the circumference of the world, and I had heard my father's stories about the Greenies in a dim nightlight-lit bedroom, storytelling will forever be to me a most intimate act: the writer's voice is inside my head, inside me. The writer's consideration for me is shown not in sparing me his shame but in rendering his story clearly—"immediately, instantaneously graspable," in Chekhov's words—so that, most paradoxically in the case of autobiography, the writer seems to disappear into the details. "Released to an outpouring," "self-forgetful in order to meet the demands of the thing seen and the thing being made," he becomes his book, the story itself.

I haven't read Kathryn Harrison's *The Kiss* or Frank McCourt's *Angela's Ashes*, but I do know that Harrison's book is "about" incest and McCourt's is "about" his impoverished childhood in Limerick with his alcoholic mother (and includes her incestuous affair with her cousin). I know this despite not watching afternoon talk shows.

This sort of sound-bite information seems to be in the air itself. Unfortunately, it's mistaken for knowledge—a natural mistake since we are forced to process so much information all the time. Humans, the learning animal, have adapted to this condition of daily life in the United States and much of the world. But it's a particularly unfortunate mistake when applied to books, although publishers encourage it and apparently believe they have to (and have to include marketing directors in their publishing decisions). Such information says less about a book than a Pepsi commercial says about Pepsi because a book is a more complicated mental and emotional experience than a soft drink, but they are now subject to the same processing mechanism, and this kind of thinking—this adaptation to infoglut—may now be the largest single obstacle between the writer and reader: it may be keeping some of the best books from being bought, published, and even written, and almost certainly affects how people read (or, more often, don't). To know Kathryn Harrison's book is about incest is to know almost nothing about it. Other books, especially fiction and poetry without identifiable and startling subjects, are less easily mistranslated into information and therefore do not enter the air at all.

This said, once a book is in a reader's hands, its relationship to him seems potentially the same as it ever was. It can teach not what to think and feel but how to think and feel. That some readers seek personal stories in reaction to a depersonalized culture in which institutional sources of authority are untrustworthy may partially account for the so-called "memoir explosion." Autobiography is only more obviously "personal" than poetry or fiction, but it is finally always about memory, and as much about the moment of recollection as the moment being recalled—the presentness of the past and the pastness of the present which every person must work out for himself over and over again if he wants a chance to be happy and useful and available to the ordinary pleasures of life. Other people's lives are interesting to us, but in this singular respect every good autobiography is also our own, a tale of the tribe that does for us what stories have always done.

AUTHENTICITY AND AUTHORITY

I n *Out of Africa*, Isak Dinesen described the Kikuyu tribe's first exposure to writing:

> I learned that the effect of a piece of news was many times magnified when it was imparted by writing. The messages that would be received with doubt and scorn if they had been given by word of mouth were now taken as gospel truth.

—whereas *we* may have just weathered the cultural moment when erudite critical theorists devoted their best energy to "liberating the signifier from the signified," as if written discourse were actually a kind of Mad Hatter's tea party. Writers were the casualty of this campaign, replaced by what Michel Foucault called "the author function." As Frederick Crews said in *The Critics Bear It Away,*

> Once writers have been discounted as the primary shapers of their works, critics are free to "liberate signifiers from the signified"— that is, to make a text mean anything or nothing according to whim.

As an operative author function myself, I'm reminded of a graffito I used to see carved into desktops when I was an undergraduate at Notre Dame:

"God is dead."—Nietzsche, 1899
"Nietzsche is dead."—God, 1900

We could do the same now for Foucault, but, as Nixon said, it would be wrong. Moreover, if we liberate Foucault's signifier it does indeed signify something: the decline in the prestige of writing from its dazzling introduction into preliterate culture to its diminished role in our own. There is no question about that. If the prestige of writing is diminished—not by the collective failure of writers but by the once-again dazzling new technologies of communication and memory, which are changing (just as writing did) the very nature of human communication and memory—the prestige of writers, wizards of the old technology, is diminished. Not surprisingly, this makes writers anxious. It impinges on their livelihood, on what they can publish, and on what they write. It's impossible to know where we are going. We could end up in broom closets wearing virtual reality helmets and blinking across the galaxy at one another. Perhaps artfully.

The two incontrovertible lessons of the history of technologies—the things humans invent to alter their world—are (1) they have a momentum of their own and (2) their cultural hence psychological effects are huge and unpredictable. This is what scares people, although the effects are usually a mixed bag and occasionally unambiguously benign. Antibiotics have been swell, and we can really appreciate them now that resistant strains of bacteria have developed to make so many of them ineffective. There is no doubt that the American Revolution in 1776 would not have happened without the invention of movable type in 1452. On most days I think this was more good than bad. *War and Peace* would not have been distributed or probably even written without the steam that powered the locomotives and the presses. The ambition of Tolstoy's novels was obviously an outgrowth of his cultural and technological moment. At present, which is all I can even attempt to describe, there are and can be no more Tolstoys: writers who immediately and significantly affect their society's political and cultural life, which in turn affects their writing and indeed all writing. There is certainly something in this to mourn. When Chekhov heard Tolstoy was seriously ill, he wrote:

> I dread Tolstoy's death. If he died, a large vacuum would be formed in my life. In the first place, I have never loved any human being

as much as I do him. I am an unbeliever, but of all faiths I regard his as the one nearest to me and the one that suits me best. Second, when Tolstoy is part of literature, it is easy and agreeable to be a writer; even the knowledge that you have not accomplished and never will accomplish anything is not so terrible, for Tolstoy makes up for all of us. His activity justifies all the hopes and expectations that are pinned on literature. Third, Tolstoy, with his enormous authority, stands firm, and as long as he remains among the living, bad taste in literature, all vulgarity, insolent or tearful, all harsh, embittered vanities, will remain remote and in deep shadow. Only his moral authority is capable of keeping so-called literary moods and trends at a certain height. Without him, it would all be a flock without a shepherd, or a jumble in which it would be hard to find one's way.

With a nod to Foucault, I must say that this homage says no less about Chekhov's great spirit than it does about Tolstoy's great work, but it seems unlikely that we will be hearing any such tributes to Michael Crichton or Danielle Steele. Nor are they our cultural movers and shakers. The real money guys, directors like Spielberg and Stone, make the real blockbusters, like *Schindler's List* and *JFK* (the latter of which caused a new congressional hearing on Kennedy's assassination). We live in a different world than Chekhov's and speak a language into which it's hard to translate phrases like "moral authority." Both of these movies did have the effects they did in part because of their moral thrust, but they were and are impossible to watch (for me, at least) without an awareness that that moral thrust is part of the product. Corporations do not have moral authority, as much as their spokesmen may want us to think so. Only humans do. Both must be known by their actions, not by their spin doctors. In Spielberg's case, especially, it was essential for him to appear earnest, which was the business of his PR director and media coach. The possibility that he may in fact be earnest in his own mind does not in the least alter the fact that his movie is not, which is the only evidence that matters. Schlock pervades everything in his *Schindler's List* from the shape of the narrative to the characterizations. There isn't a moment when Spielberg isn't looking at the audience instead of at his material, and the places he departs most egregiously from Thomas Keneally's novel—such as Schindler's weepy speech at the end—are dead giveaways. Everything in the movie is just a whole lot too pretty. When the women strip to shower at the death camp, they could be heading for the jacuzzi at Sports Club LA. To tell the truth about the Holocaust the way Primo Levi does in *Survival in Auschwitz* is not a viable corporate decision. In arguments about the movie I had with my friends, some of them forgave it on that basis. This makes me apoplectic, since reducing what we ask is one of the main symptoms of media drubbing—a Gresham's Law of aesthetic response, bad money driving out the good, producing one standard for "art" and another for "entertainment."

The brain, God help us, apparently registers every experience. Neurobiologists are now arguing over the best metaphor for what happens when we register an experience in memory; the dominant one at present is that the *volume* of certain synapses is turned up. That is, among the trillions of pathways in our brains the billions of neurons can take, a memory makes it easier for that pathway to be taken again, as if the neuron were attracted to the synapse that clamors loudest for it. This seems like an unconsciously positive and self-justifying description of our infoglut culture, as was the survival of the fittest for nineteenth-century British colonialism. The average teenager (wherever he is) watches six hours of television a day and he will see an estimated two-and-a-half million commercials if he lives to be sixty-five, not to mention the ads in newspapers and magazines and on almost every item of clothing he and his friends wear. What is this doing to people? Nobody really knows. Our brains are exposed to those whose only job is to profit from them, who bewilder and enchant us. But this is almost beside the point. The point is only a person can have moral authority and the evidence of it is spoken by the art, whatever its form. It's not that movies or TV programs can't have it; its simply that they don't when every decision from casting to camera angles (not to mention what the story is and how it's told) is made to make money, not to tell the truth. Everybody knows this and yet the idea of truth itself is consequently and continually undermined. We who agree on nothing agree that there is no such thing. The champion platitude of our time is that we each have our own points of view. This is also just a whole lot too obvious. For a writer, it has to be the starting point not the finish line.

Here's Chekhov again:

> A writer should be as objective as a chemist; he must give up everyday subjectivity and realize that dunghills play a very respectable role in a landscape, and that evil passions belong to life as much as good ones do.

> A writer is not a confectioner, not a cosmetician, not an entertainer; he is a man with an obligation, under contract to his duty, his conscience; he must do what he has set out to do; he is bound to fight his squeamishness and dirty his imagination with what is dirty in life.

> Literature is called artistic when it depicts life as it actually is. Its purpose is truth, honest and indisputable.

Survival in Auschwitz clearly embodies Levi's intention is to tell the truth. The importance of intention, much less of telling the truth, has been a taboo topic since the New Critics (who taught Bishop's and Welty's generation how to read and consequently how to write) decreed that to identify the writer's intention was a fallacy. They did so in order to focus exclusively on how the writing works. Like many good ideas, this one merged with others floating in the air (from symbolism and surrealism) and evolved into a misconception: that the writer shouldn't have any intention in the first place. Chekhov said:

> If one is to deny that question and intention exist in creative work, it becomes necessary to admit that the artist creates without premeditation, without design, under the influence of an affect; therefore, if some author were to boast to me that he had written a tale without a previously thought out intention but by inspiration alone, I would call him a madman.

This is not to argue that there isn't discovery and a sense of play in the process of composition—just that there can't be only those if the writing is not to be merely trivial or eccentric. Auden, with characteristic perspicacity, said,

> Sincerity, in the proper sense of the word, meaning authenticity, is, or ought to be, a writer's chief preoccupation. . . . Some writers confuse authenticity, which they ought always to aim at, with originality, which they should never bother about.

Like happiness, originality comes as a byproduct. To seek it, to will it, is the best way not to get it. As for authenticity, we are dying for it amidst all the fakery and fragmentation. It's a reason to read and a reason to write—for me, the compelling reason—and directs every decision about both subject and style.

Authenticity ("that which can be believed or accepted") suffuses the writing of *Survival in Auschwitz* in its every aspect: its absence of sentimentality and self-pity, the rigor of its self-portrayal, its compassion for others, the efficient arc of the narrative, the unobtrusive brilliance of its style. When I read it, as I have ten or twelve times (once aloud), I don't care in the least who Primo Levi was except as the writer of this book. But in this capacity I care absolutely. Henry James said, "What interests me most about a work of art is the artist's quality of mind." I would add to "mind": spirit, heart, talent (Chekhov: "Talent is the ability to distinguish the essential from the inessential"). Levi's writing tells me who Levi is. He is not Primo the character in the book. He *is* the book. In Flaubert's famous words, "The writer in his book is like God in the universe, present everywhere and visible nowhere." It doesn't matter that Levi wrote his book on Sunday afternoons over the course of a single year, or threw himself from the fourth floor down the central stairwell of his apartment building forty years later, or had a wife and two children, or loved his mother, or was a tiny matchstick of a man with a short pointy beard, or might have done some things he was ashamed of. The book speaks with moral authority across the distance of more than fifty years in a translation from another language. There may be people who do not love it. Happily, I have not met them. The three times I taught the book, none of my students were so unkind or impolitic to tell me they didn't love it. But when it was published in 1947 the memory of the war in Italy was painfully fresh. It sold a few hundred copies and went out of print.

Here is a passage from the chapter entitled "October 1944," which dramatizes one of the periodic selections of prisoners to be gassed. There was more than one selection in Auschwitz during the year of Levi's imprisonment, but this is the one that stands for them all in his book. Everything about the writing is designed to allow us to see what happens as through a skylight, to understand it as the writer does in the moment he is writing, and to be inside the experience with him as a character—all at the same time. This is something movies will never be able to do, for all their power of immediacy. Levi's writing, too, could not be more transparent, and the rigor and simplicity of the style implicitly communicate the writer's understanding of what he's writing about. Note the verb tenses and the pronouns; notice where Levi positions himself both as a character in the story and as the writer who tells it and comments on it.

> Now we are all in the *Tagesraum*, and besides there being no time, there is not even any room in which to be afraid. The feeling of the warm flesh pressing all around is unusual and not unpleasant. One has to take care to hold up one's nose so as to breathe, and not to crumple or lose the card in one's hand.
>
> The *Blockaltester* has closed the connecting-door and has opened the other two which lead from the dormitory and the *Tagesraum* outside. Here, in front of the two doors, stands the arbiter of our fate, an ss subaltern. On his right is the *Blockaltester,* on his left, the quartermaster of the hut. Each one of us, as he comes naked out of the *Tagesraum* into the cold October air, has to run the few steps between the two doors, give the card to the ss man and enter the dormitory door. The ss man, in the fraction of second between two successive crossings, with a glance at one's back and front, judges everyone's fate, and in turn gives the card to the man on his right or his left, and this is the life or death of each of us. In three or four minutes, a hut of two hundred men is "done," as is the whole camp of twelve thousand men in the course of an afternoon.

Jammed in the charnel-house of the *Tagesraum,* I gradually felt the human pressure around me slacken, and in a short time it was my turn. Like everyone, I passed by with a brisk and elastic step, trying to hold my head high, my chest forward and my muscles contracted and conspicuous. With the corner of my eye I tried to look behind my shoulders, and my card seemed to end on the right.

As we gradually come back into the dormitory we are allowed to dress ourselves. Nobody yet knows with certainty his own fate, it has first of all to be established whether the condemned cards were on the right or on the left. By now there is no longer any point in sparing each other's feelings with superstitious scruples. Everybody crowds around the oldest, the most wasted-away, the most "musselmann"; if their cards went to the left, the left is certainly the side of the condemned.

Even before the selection is over, everybody knows that the left was effectively the *"schlechte Seite,"* the bad side. There have naturally been some irregularities: Rene, for example, so young and robust, ended on the left; perhaps it was because he has glasses, perhaps because he walks a little stooped like a myope, but more probably because of a simple mistake: Rene passed the commission immediately in front of me and there could have been a mistake with our cards. I think about it, discuss it with Alberto, and we agree that the hypothesis is probable; I do not know what I will think tomorrow and later; today I feel no distinct emotion.

There is of course a great tradition behind this style. As Francis-Noel Thomas and Mark Turner write in *Clear and Simple as the Truth,* "The classic writer, no matter how abstract his subject, will present it as so sharply defined in itself and so independent of the writer as to count for all of us as a 'thing.'" They argue cogently that a style is based on certain assumptions and decisions, that it has implicit meaning as well as communicates meaning, that it isn't superfluous or superficial. Classic style "rests on the assumption that it is impossible to think disinterestedly, to know the results of disinterested thought, and to present them without fundamental distortion"—in other words, that "truth can be known." This is why for Chekhov the writer must give up "everyday subjectivity" and "be as objective as a chemist" (Levi was a chemist by profession), and what he meant in this compliment to Gorky: "When you depict a thing you see it and feel it with your hands. This is true art." It's also what Frost meant when he said, "A subject has to be held clear outside of me with struts and as it were set up for an object. A subject must be an object." It must be because this is the writer's duty and discipline. It's what saves his work, from even himself. It's what makes it authentic and valuable to others.

Thomas and Turner's fine observation about Mark Twain's *Life on the Mississippi* also applies to *Survival in Auschwitz:*

> The experiences Twain presents are not private; had you been there, you would have seen what he saw and his job is to put you in a position to see exactly that. . . . In this way, Twain the writer and Twain the possessor of entirely personal experiences are never allowed to displace the subject—life on the Mississippi. Twain the boy and Twain the steamboatman are part of that subject, and are presented as such.

Never allowed to displace the subject: in Levi's case, the subject is survival in Auschwitz. His action in writing of putting this subject ahead of himself, of giving it precedence, says implicitly and constantly that he believes what happened there is more important than what happened to him. He tells us what happened to him because it is necessary to his telling what happened. Because the subject is so powerful, so annihilating ("which nothing at all in the power of man can ever clean again"), Levi's action-in-writing is extremely powerful, and it's the source of the writing's authority (the Latin root of which means "to enlarge"). The reader is enlarged by *it,* the act of witnessing, by what the writer *does*. This enactment of his intention to tell the truth is far more beautiful and noble than any explicit expression of beautiful sentiments or noble convictions, which are in any case usually suspect. In Spielberg's interpolated saccharine scene at the end of *Schindler's List,* such sentiments are there to make us think Nice Guy

Sensitive Fellow Good Person. For Levi, they would represent a debasement of moral intelligence—his moral intelligence in action, and ours as we experience it and are enlarged by it.

No matter what the political or cultural or personal conditions, there have always been writers who have been able to write with an authenticity that is permanently valuable to others and immediately necessary to the writer him- or herself. Tolstoy certainly did it in his fiction and he certainly did not in his crackpot tracts about agriculture, politics, and personal hygiene, which often had more widespread and instantaneous effect. There are the dramatic examples of Mandelstam in his prison cell and Dickinson in her bedroom, Keats and Chekhov dying of tuberculosis, Berryman and Faulkner in alcoholic despair, and Plath furiously and fruitlessly trying to write her way back to the desire to live. Some of these are heroic; all are moving and useful if clearly understood. I've tried to imagine how Levi must have felt having written a great book if ever there was one and having it ignored for almost ten years until the world was ready for it. There are CD-ROMs full of such examples, but it's still a fatal error to sentimentalize writers' lives into a hagiolatry of the cultural victimization of the writer's superior, more sensitive being, because this is a form of "everyday subjectivity," self-pity, and mush-mindedness that infects writing and kills it. I believe it's part of the task of being writers at present to resist this intently and intentionally in what we have been told is becoming a "post-literate" culture in which we "post-moderns" are "post-humanists." We ain't post-nothin'. We are really here. Undead and loving it.

Since I have used Chekhov's letters as my main guide through this moral minefield, I want to end with advice he wrote to his wife in 1899 while he was trying to regain his health in Yalta and she was acting in Moscow:

> Art, and especially the stage, is an endeavor in which stumbling is unavoidable. There will be many unsuccessful days ahead, many entirely unsuccessful seasons, there will be great misunderstandings and deep disappointments and you have to be ready for all

that, you have to expect it, and despite it all you must stubbornly, fanatically do what you think is right.

No matter how things change, they stay the same. It is a sign of our times and maybe of any time that Chekhov's *Letters,* also one of the great books if ever there was one, is currently out of print.* You can't buy it in any translation. But you can probably find it in the library.

---

* Two paperbacks in print contain tiny samplings: *Chekhov and His Times* (A. Turkov, ed., University of Arkansas Press, 1995); *The Portable Chekhov* (A. Yarmolinsky, ed., Viking, 1947). The best editions in English taken together contain about 5 percent of the more than four thousand letters available in Russian; these editions were published coincidentally in the same year: *Chekhov's Letters* (Yarmolinsky, ed., Viking, 1973); *The Letters of Anton Chekhov* (Karlinsky and Heim, eds., Harper & Row, 1973). The latter went out of print in paperback in 1996, when my essay was written. It has since been reissued by Northwestern University Press under the title *Chekhov's Life and Thought.*

VOCATION ACCORDING TO DICKINSON

Despite her notorious slant tellings, proverbs, paradoxes, riddles, enigmas, deflections, self-protections, and indirections, Dickinson is first to last and above all earnest. Sincerity was to her a supreme value; the final measure was the Heart. "To be made alive is so chief a thing all else inevitably adds": she meant to be quintessentially alive on this earth and she most certainly was. This was her greatest success. Her poems are its instruments and products. Her genius, as she herself defined the term, was "the ignition of affection—not intellect, as it is supposed—the exaltation of devotion, and in proportion our capacity for that, is our experience of genius." Her capacity for the "exaltation of devotion" was extraordinary. The devotion she exalted was to friends, family, loved ones, the natural world, home, "sermons on unbelief," books, and—especially—poetry: poetry that made her feel as if the top of her head were taken off, reading it where she could find it in Shakespeare, Keats, Herbert, the Brownings, the Book of Revelation, the Psalms, the Gospel of Matthew, and also—very luckily for us—writing it herself. Writing poems was life-sustaining, even life-creating. It created the place in which she fully experienced her experience. What she made in her poems she used in her life. The process of writing and all it involved grew her soul. It was a spiritual discipline, the lifelong practice of a craft, and an entertainment. When, after a few years out of touch, Higginson asked if she was still writing, she responded, "I have no other Playmate." The idea that either poetry or religion was separable from life was repugnant to her.

Art for art's sake would have struck her as a ludicrous, debased idea. The foundation and purpose of art was moral and religious, as it was for every poet of her time except Poe, but, unlike the Victorian sages, for her the relationship between art and morality was implicit not explicit, private not social, neither pious nor privileged but enmeshed with gritty, difficult, daily life, and every crack and crease in their connections was open to exploration. God ("I know him but a little") was not so much to be praised as called into account for human suffering, including her own, but her own only as a representative, "a supposed person." (She reminded Higginson, "When I state myself, as the Representative of the Verse—it does not mean—me—but a supposed person.") She is often playfully and affectionately ironic (she was known locally for her wit and humor), but the few scornful words of hers that have survived are directed at fops, atheists, liars, seekers of fame, and women who regard themselves as "soft creatures." "'Tis a dangerous moment for any one when the meaning goes out of things and Life stands straight—and punctual—and yet no content(s) (signal) comes(s). Yet such moments are. If we survive them they expand us, if we do not, but that is Death, whose if is everlasting": Open your eyes, she says again and again, "the heaven below" is right here right now right in front of you, despite grief and loss so intense it threatens madness. "O Vision of Language": all one has to do is see—or, more accurately, as she wrote it, "see to see -".

What prevented seeing, and feeling, and thinking, she believed, were the conventions of society, religion, and language itself, including the conventions of poetry as it was practiced in mid-nineteenth-century America. "Convention" is one of those pale words with a calm face that conceals a blinding force. "Convention" means an agreement, a social agreement, but such agreements are institutionalized, internalized, mistaken for truth, and enforced by shunning and shame. They are part of the fabric of identity, threatening to question, almost invisible in their deep weave. They make social interaction possible but social interaction torqued by worldly power. Emily Dickinson's father was the most prominent citizen of Amherst. He brought the railroad to Amherst. He was a United States Congressman when Emily was in her mid-twenties, a delegate to the Whig

Presidential Convention, the treasurer of Amherst College, and a member of the Congregational Church. His father bankrupted himself starting Amherst College as a bastion of Puritanism against the defections of Yale and Harvard. Emily was schooled at Amherst Academy and Mount Holyoke Seminary, where subjects such as Rhetoric (in which she became most expert) were taught in the light of faith by teachers whose contract of employment required them to be of upstanding character and instruct their students according to accepted teachings of the Bible. Her family owned nineteen Bibles. When she was fourteen, her father presented her with one of her own, and a piano for which she bound sheet music of waltzes, marches, and quicksteps for the many jolly social evenings with her friends. Most of her closest friends and all of her family except herself joined the Congregational Church by answering the call of Christ in the religious revivals that swept through Amherst during her teenage years. She heard over fifteen hundred sermons by the time she was twenty-one. That year (1851) her sister recorded in her diary hundreds of social calls the two Dickinson sisters made and received. Puritanism was in her blood and in the air she breathed. The independence of spirit it took to resist these pressures of conformity is paradoxically itself a legacy of the Puritans, who emigrated from England to practice their own faith and think their own thoughts. But the severe doctrines of Calvinism had a social component, especially the doctrine of predestined election evident in a person's behavior, including what he said and especially what he said at the moment of death. If the last words of the dying person were calm and accepting, they were taken as a sign of his election to heaven and inspiration to the living. It was the duty of teenage girls in Amherst to tend the very ill and the death-watch itself was a religious ritual. It's no wonder that death etched Emily Dickinson's consciousness and informed her writing. She was in the presence of death all her life, not insulated from it the way most of us are now. The house she lived in until she was twenty-five bordered the village graveyard and she could watch funeral processions enter the main gate from the north windows. "Life is death we're lengthy at, death the hinge to life." About her own death, she wavered between its "Everlasting if" and a belief in immortality, which she called her "Flood subject." Death for the supposed person in some of her greatest poems is rendered as a moment of transition from life to afterlife, narrated retrospectively, as if the boldness of the imaginative leap was itself so compelling it created the truth. About the death of loved ones, she was unambiguous: it was the worst thing in the world. The onset of her final illness from Bright's disease (which shuts down the kidneys) she herself believed was caused by the successive deaths of her "closest earthly friend," Reverend Charles Wadsworth, her mother, her twelve-year-old nephew Gilbert, and her beloved Judge Lord: "The doctor calls it 'revenge of the nerves'; but who but Death had wronged them?" It was in the middle of this onslaught in 1883 that she had the courage to write, "To have been made alive is so chief a thing, all else inevitably adds." Adding: "Were it not riddled by partings, it were too divine."

At these polarities of bliss and anguish and the gradations between, she wrote. Much myth and mystery has been made of what Richard Sewall calls her "withdrawal" from society, climaxing, we can hope, with Julie Harris's embarrassing "Belle of Amherst" and Sandra Gilbert and Susan Gubar's absurd reduction of her into "a helpless agoraphobic, trapped in a room in her father's house." Emily Dickinson was anything but helpless. She wrote to her cousin nursing a dying friend: "Of the 'thorn,' dear, give it to me, for I am strongest. Never carry what I can carry, for though I think I bend, something straightens me." After her death, her brother Austin wrote in *The Springfield Republican:* "She was full of courage—but always had a peculiar personal sensitiveness. She saw things directly and just as they were. She abhorred sham and cheapness." According to his own report, when Higginson asked her "if she never felt want of employment, never going off the place & never seeing any visitor," she responded, "I never thought of conceiving that I could ever have the slightest approach to such a want in all future time" (and added) "I feel that I have not expressed myself strongly enough." Anyone who reads her poetry even superficially might sense the spiritual strength and supreme artistic control it takes to witness clearly the tumultuous emotional extremes she renders with laser precision, but here in Freud's century, where spirituality has been reduced to psychology, forestsful of trees have died for books to explain "psychoanalytically" her decision to pursue a vocation that she herself plainly saw according to the word's definition in her 1841 edition of Noah Webster's lexicon: a divine calling to a religious life ("religious" and "life" being for her almost a redundancy). "Let Emily sing for you because she cannot pray," she wrote to her young cousins orphaned by their father's death, and included a poem in the letter. It is no accident that the form she adapted for virtually all of her poems was a liturgical form not a literary form, the hymn not the sonnet or blank verse her admired Keats set himself to master. Poetry was prayer for Emily Dickinson, especially the poems least like conventional prayers. Her vocation was to write them and write she did: in her less than thirty years of working life at least 1,789 poems and we-don't-know-how-many letters, at least some of which she also composed in drafts. Johnson's three-volume edition of her letters, with introduction, notes, appendices, and index, is 1,046 letters and 999 pages long, and this, according to the best scholarly estimate, is five percent of them. That would make it twenty thousand letters and thirty to thirty-five books of poems (at fifty to sixty poems per book), not counting fragments found among her papers at her death. Let's call it on the average a book of poems and five hundred letters a year. Of this remarkable lifetime of work, Dickinson herself wrote in 1882: "The little sentences I began and never finished—the little wells I dug and never filled—," which reminds me of Beethoven lamenting on his deathbed that he had only accomplished a crumb of what he had intended, only Dickinson's lament is so much humbler and quieter.

It was of course not only the time to do this work that Emily Dickinson's "withdrawal" gained for herself but also the focus. Her famous white dresses might have been a uniform like a policeman's or priest's: when she put one on it reminded her of her job, her duty, and who she had to be to do it. Wearing the traditional white as a symbol of purity and fidelity can be found as at least as early as the Book of Revelation, her favorite book of the Bible, which her friend from adolescence Joseph Lyman quoted in a letter in about 1857: "And they shall walk with me in white: for they are worthy." She herself writes in the first months of 1862 (307 [#271]):

A solemn thing - it was - I said
A woman - white - to be -
And wear - if God should count me fit -
Her blameless mystery -

A hallowed thing - to drop a life
Into the purple well -
Too plummetless - that it return -
Eternity - until

I pondered how the bliss would look -
And would it feel as big -
When I could take it in my hand -
As hovering - seen - through fog -

And then - the size of this "small" life -
The Sages - call it small -
Swelled - like Horizons - in my vest -
And I sneered - softly - "small"! *

Doesn't sound so helpless, does it? The year of Lyman's letter, when
Emily was twenty-seven, seems to have been the year she said the
"solemn thing . . . / A woman - white - to be" that committed her to
her vocation as a poet that swelled like Horizons in her vest and expanded her vision and her life. The same year (1857) marked the publication of her copy of *The Imitation of Christ* by Thomas à Kempis,
which Austin's wife and Emily's intimate friend and next-door neigh-
bor, Sue Gilbert Dickinson, gave to her (Sue gave her another in 1876).
It is a powerful fifteenth-century redaction of Scripture, a how-to
book to achieve inner peace by living a rigorous, uncompromised
spiritual life. The chapter entitled "On the Love of Solitude and Si-

---

*The texts and numbers of Emily Dickinson's poems are from *The Complete Poems of
Emily Dickinson: Variorum Edition,* edited by R. W. Franklin (Harvard University Press,
1998). The numbers in brackets are from *The Complete Poems of Emily Dickinson,* edited
by Thomas H. Johnson (Little Brown and Co., 1960)—the standard edition until superseded by Franklin's.

lence" in Dickinson's copy of the book is heavily marked, including this sentence: "The greatest saints avoided the society of men, when they could conveniently, and did rather choose to live in God, in secret." Shortly thereafter or about the same time, Dickinson wrote the first of her eerie Master letters and began keeping the fascicles, four or five sheets folded and "stab-bound" containing eighteen to twenty poems each. Thirty-nine of these were found after her death and twenty-five others not threaded. They are fair copies of the poems, not drafts, and all the dating has been done on the basis of the handwriting matching letters in which she sometimes, as in the letter to her cousins, would copy a poem into the text of the letter as if suddenly breaking into verse, although the letters and poems were composed separately and she sometimes sent the same poem to different correspondents. Franklin dates an astonishing 887 poems between 1858 and 1864, when she apparently stopped making the fascicles, with 229 more poems in 1865. That is a poem almost every other day, including many of her best ones. These are almost all fair copies. The drafts that remain are often just tiny scraps of paper, two-line units, many of them aphoristic; in some instances, two scraps were found fastened together by a straight pin to make a quatrain. Her mother's long illness began in 1855 and Emily with her sister, Vinnie, attended her daily; together they saw to the housework, supervising four servants, and there was a lot of it to be done for the most socially prominent family in Amherst; Emily's Rye-and-Indian bread was famous (her specialty was baking); she tended her large garden in the backyard and, until her dog Carlo died, took him for long walks in the countryside in late afternoon when the weather was fine. But obviously she was composing her poems all the time.

In any case, by 1862, when she wrote her now-famous initial letter to Thomas Wentworth Higginson after reading his essay "To a Young Contributor" in *The Atlantic Monthly*, she was a confident, accomplished artist committed to her vocation. Much of the Emily Dickinson myth has its source in her letters to him and his letter to his wife describing her after their first of two meetings. Higginson himself has gotten a very bad press in the last fifty years, when the extent of his and Mabel Loomis Todd's regularizing Dickinson's punctuation and phrasing for the first editions of her poems in 1891 and 1892 became known and all her letters to him were published (most of his to her were destroyed or lost). Richard Sewall's verdict has become the standard one: "As a literary advisor he failed her completely." Dickinson's own estimate of his value to her was exactly the opposite. She wrote to Higginson in 1869: "Of our greatest acts we are ignorant—You were not aware that you saved my Life." What she meant by this becomes clearer if we understand that her life depended on her vocation (and vice versa). In 1877, she wrote, "Often, when troubled by entreaty, that paragraph of your's [from 'To a Young Contributor' which provoked her first letter] has saved me—'Such being the Majesty of the Art you presume to practice, you can at least take time before dishonoring it,' and Enobarbus said, 'Leave that which leaves itself.'" The troubling "entreaty" to which she refers might be either entreaty by others for her time and attention or an entreaty from that part of the self that wants the work to go faster and better than it does— although it's hard to imagine her work going faster and better than it did. In either case, Higginson's admonition—"Such being the Majesty of the Art you presume to practice, you can at least take time before dishonoring it"—read positively, as she had the grace to read it, counsels devotion to the art, and it was this devotion and the exaltation of this devotion that sustained her and swelled the Horizons in her vest. As for "Leave that which leaves itself" (actually "Let that be left / Which leaves itself" spoken by Antony, not Enobarbus, in Shakespeare's play), she may have meant removing herself from the demands of people who are spiritually bankrupt or maybe something like what she wrote to Higginson also in 1877 after his wife died: "Do not try to be saved—but let Redemption find you—as it certainly will—Love is its own rescue, for we—at our supremest, are but its trembling Emblems—." In either case, on the latter occasion, fifteen years after first contacting him, it is her turn to counsel active patience, the willingness to wait, which is also part of devotion, both to art and to God.

She had chosen Higginson carefully to ask to be her "preceptor." He was a graduate of Harvard Divinity School, an ordained but unorthodox minister, a firebrand abolitionist, a sponsor of John Brown's raids in Kansas and at Harper's Ferry, a suffragist, a spiritualist, a translator of Epictetus, and a famous man of letters, loosely associated with Emerson's circle of Transcendentalists. She claimed to have read every word he wrote. For fours years (since 1858) she had been reading his *Atlantic Monthly* essays on nature, which she particularly loved. They are much influenced by Emerson and Thoreau, and the belief, as Emerson put it, "in the existence of the material world as an expression of the spiritual or real" and that "particular natural facts are symbols of particular spiritual facts," a conviction Dickinson herself sometimes shared and sometimes didn't. ("We both believe and disbelieve a hundred times an hour, which keeps Believing nimble.") This is her initial letter to Higginson, dated April 15, 1862, shortly before he was appointed Colonel of the First South Carolina Volunteers, the first regiment of freed slaves to serve in the Union Army:

> Mr Higginson,
> Are you too deeply occupied to say if my Verse is alive?
> The Mind is so near itself—it cannot see, distinctly—and I have none to ask—
> Should you think it breathed—and had you the leisure to tell me, I should feel quick gratitude—
> If I make the mistake—that you dared to tell me ["Such be the Majesty etc."]—would give me sincerer honor—toward you—
> I enclose my name—asking you, if you please—Sir—to tell me what is true?
> That you will not betray me—it is needless to ask—since Honor is it's own pawn—

She enclosed a card with her name on it and four poems, none nearly her best, the best-known of which is "Safe in their Alabaster Chambers." "Tell me what is *true*," "Should you think it *breathed*," "Are you too deeply occupied to say if my Verse is *alive*": "*true, breathing, alive*": this is what she wants her poems to be. She wants to bring language alive on the page through the power of truth ("A Book is only the Heart's Portrait - every Page a Pulse -"). To do this it was first necessary for her to begin to withdraw from the inevitable judgment of people in society, including the society of the church. She may have felt that her extraordinary, even exhausting love for people (what she called "a sweet wolf within us that demands its food") made her particularly susceptible to their influence. Like most of us, she is a somewhat different person depending on whom she is writing a letter to. Her poems, however, are an absolute communication, timeless, to no one and to everyone, one person at a time. It's estimated that she sent more than 650 of them to people in letters, about 250 next door to Sue, whose criticism she greatly valued and used when their intimate rocky relationship did not prevent it. But publishing her poems would have created a scandal for her family, and anyway, in her view, their public success would have been equally fatal to her and therefore killed her ability to write them. About the effect of fame she does not tell it slant at all. She could hardly be more unambiguous, unwavering, and blunt:

> Renown perceives itself
> And that degrades the Flower -
> The Daisy that has looked behind
> Has compromised its power -

Fame is inherently dishonorable, a "bubble," "a fickle food," a Bee with a sting and a wing; publication is "the auction of the mind of man," "so foul a thing" that reduces "the Human Spirit / To Disgrace of Price -". Significantly, these remarks are from poems no one else may have seen during her lifetime. To Higginson, in response to his apparently unsolicited suggestion that she "delay to publish," she is much more gentle and ironic:

> I smiled when you suggest I delay "to publish"—that being foreign to my thought, as Firmament to Fin—
> If fame belonged to me, I could not escape her—if she did not, the longest day would pass me on the chase—and the approbation of my Dog, would forsake me—then—My Barefoot-Rank is better—

"Barefoot-rank": that is, a buck private with no shoes in comparison to *Colonel* Higginson. It's better, she believed, because it was the only way she could write the poems she wrote, because "renown" necessarily "perceives itself," thus changing the person who writes. Whatever your own opinion about this for yourself happens to be, it was unquestionably the only way Emily Dickinson believed she could write the truth that gives her poems life. ("Truth is such a *rare* thing it is delightful to tell it.") Plus her dog continued to approve of her, which of course is to say herself. Nor, she says, are her long days lost chasing fame. "Firmament" may be higher, but "Fin" thrives in an entirely different element, one deeper and more mysterious. She never looks over her shoulder at the reader, never looks behind and compromises her power.

This is how Flannery O'Connor articulated this discipline: "[Jacques] Maritain says that to produce a work of art requires 'the constant attention of the purified mind,' and the business of the purified mind in this case is to see that those elements of the personality that don't bear on the subject at hand are excluded. . . . Everything has to be subordinated to a whole which is not you." This is what Dickinson did in poem after poem. They are stripped of incidentals. Anecdote is relentlessly sifted to its ulterior purpose. There is almost never a detail that doesn't *work,* having been subject to the scrutiny of that purified mind, heart, and spirit that made the poem. "There is a pain - so utter - / It swallows substance up - "; "One Blessing had I than the rest / So larger to my Eyes / That I stopped gauging - satisfied - / For this enchanted size - ": She doesn't tell you what *her* pain or *her* blessing was. For her personally, the utter pain might have been stubbing her toe or the largest blessing a big bowl of ice cream. Our identification with the speaker is not interfered with by contingencies: no dross in this "alloyless" "introspective Mine." She's not in the least interested in complaining or rejoicing or even in particular incidents but in their effects—in other words, in how it feels to be a living human being, across the whole range of human feeling from "a perfect - paralyzing Bliss" to "that White Sustenance - / Despair -". This, I think, is one of her most valuable lessons for working poets: the poem is not about you, it's about the reader.

This is also why she believes "True poems flee"—the poem is in the reader's feeling and feeling is momentary. "Consciousness is the only home of which we *now* know" and, again, "We both believe and

disbelieve a hundred times an hour, which keeps Believing nimble."
In all of her poems about poetry and poets, the poetry is an action
and the poet is merely the stimulus to the action, even if in perform-
ing this action he becomes "Himself - to Him - a Fortune - / Exterior - to Time -". In "The Poets light but Lamps," by the time we
come to "their" in the seventh line (which, by the way, marks a very
unusual line-break for Dickinson), it has accumulated the referents
"Poets," "Wicks," and "Suns," from the small and close to the large
and distant, from dark to daylight.

> The Poets light but Lamps -
> Themselves - go out -
> The Wicks they stimulate -
> If vital Light
>
> Inhere as do the Suns -
> Each Age a Lens
> Disseminating their
> Circumference -
>> 930 [#883] (1865)
>
> To pile like Thunder to it's close
> Then crumble grand away
> While Everything created hid
> This - would be Poetry -
>
> Or Love - the two coeval come -
> We both and neither prove -
> Experience either and consume -
> For None see God and live -
>> 1353 [#1247] (1875)

"Poetry - // Or Love - the two coeval come - / We both and neither
prove -". We prove both: neither poetry nor love exists without us
humans; we prove neither: both poetry and love exist without us as
individuals. Experience (she commands us) either love or poetry and
you will consume everything and be consumed, "For None see God

and live -". The experience of love and poetry are nothing less than the experience of God—for the poet as well as the reader.

This little poem is one of Dickinson's most heady and runic. It requires the reader's participation to interpret it, but, at least until the seventh line, the difficulty is more in what is being said than in how it's being said. It's remarkable that she is able to cast both poems in the present tense and make even a poem of ideas immediate. She almost always focuses tightly on the moment (also a great lesson for working poets), whether it be the moment of the continuous present ("There's a certain Slant of light, / Winter Afternoons-") or a specific moment of a narrative:

I heard a Fly buzz - when I died -
The Stillness in the Room
Was like the Stillness in the Air -
Between the Heaves of Storm -

The Eyes around - had wrung them dry -
And Breaths were gathering firm
For that last Onset - when the King
Be witnessed - in the Room -

I willed my Keepsakes - Signed away
What portion of me be
Assignable - and then it was
There interposed a Fly -

With Blue - uncertain stumbling Buzz -
Between the light - and me -
And then the Windows failed - and then
I could not see to see -

591 [#465] (1863)

If I had to pick one of her poems as my favorite, which happily I don't, this would be it. What a great piece of writing it is. I'm awestruck each time I read it by the shift to the past perfect tense at the beginning of the second stanza ("The Eyes around - *had* wrung

them dry"), a brilliant little shift backward in time to the few moments before the death of the speaker so she can recapitulate the
story and populate the setting with the deathwatchers and the willing
of the keepsakes and give us her wry joke about it ("Signed away /
What portion of me be / Assignable"). The joke rings a chord with
the irony of hearing a fly buzz at the moment of death and reminds
us that we're not just in the story but in the presence of someone
telling it. Also buried in that little efficient joke is the assertion that
there's a portion of her that's *not* assignable, which is the portion
(since she's dead) that is telling the story—what, for lack of a better
term, would usually be called the soul. "And then it was . . . ": The
moment generally described in the first line of the poem ("I heard a
Fly buzz - when I died") is now dramatized: the fly's "blue uncertain
stumbling buzz"—three adjectives in a row in a poem that has few
others—interposes between the reader and the forward motion of
the narrative (since the action is carried through nouns and verbs)
just as the fly in the story interposed between the speaker and the
light. This gives *us* the experience of "interposed." The spatial and
temporal experience referred to *by* the words is rendered though the
sequence *of* the words fixed into form. "And then . . . and then . . ."
(the last two lines of the poem): the story continues. "And then the
Windows failed - and then / I could not see to see -". The final miraculous move is to turn the irony itself on its ear. This ugly annoy-
ing fly is the last thing the speaker senses on earth, and, ironically,
it's what appears while the deathwatchers are expecting the King
(God) to appear. But, "then - I could not see to see -": even this lowly
creature provides a great occasion. The assertion buried here in the
poem's expert rhetoric is that this great occasion is available to us only
while we have physical eyes— only while we're alive for the sacramen-
tal act of seeing, only when we're not distracted by conventional religious ideas that call for the appearance of a grandiose God instead of
paying attention to the humble things of the earth. And of course the
larger assertion buried in the rhetoric of the narrative as a whole is
that one can tell the story of one's death after one dies. Afterlife is not
proved but enacted. Whether or not we believe in an afterlife or the

soul, we do experience them, at least to this extent. In the same letter to Higginson in which she told him he saved her life, she wrote:

> A letter always feels to me like immortality because it is the mind alone without corporeal friend. Indebted in our talk to attitude and accent, there seems a spectral power in thought that walks alone—I would like to thank you for your great kindness but never try to lift the words which I cannot hold.

In her poems, she gives them to us to hold, the moment, as she put it elsewhere, "fixed in the verse" and thereby made timeless. "Forever - is composed of Nows -" (690 [#624]). In her rendering of the moment, she discovers the divine. We are given autobiography but it is the autobiography of a soul.

After her death, Higginson published an article in the *Christian Union* in which he quoted the second stanza of "Safe in their Alabaster Chambers" and wrote, "With all its too daring concentration, it strikes a note too fine to be lost." Here's the whole poem:

Safe in their Alabaster Chambers -
Untouched by Morning -
And untouched by noon -
Lie the meek members of the Resurrection -
Rafter of Satin - and Roof of Stone -

Grand go the Years,
In the Crescent above them -
Worlds scoop their Arcs -
And Firmaments - row -
Diadems - drop
And Doges - surrender -
Soundless as Dots,
On a Disc of Snow.

124 [#216] (1859)

This is not a particularly difficult poem for us. The "concentration" was "too daring" to Higginson, judging by his own poems and the celebrated poems of the age, because the syntax is paratactic not hypotactic (that is, clauses are juxtaposed, not subordinated or restricted) and the connection between sentences is left to the reader. Higginson, for all his political vision and personal generosity, was blinded by the poetic conventions of the age, which called upon the poet to make the connections for the reader using hypotactic syntax that made the argument and moral of the poem explicit. To our taste, most of these poems sound like lectures. They are not nearly intimate enough to seem true. They seem to us to move very slowly. Although we have seen how brilliantly Emily Dickinson buries her assertions rhetorically, her poems are not arguments but experiences. Making the connections makes the reader participate in the experience. That is how she makes the poem breathe. The breath is the reader's.

We are of course used to her parataxis because of the direction poetry has taken since she died. Ezra Pound said in his 1914 "Vorticism" essay that putting one thing next to another establishes their own relationship, and out of this montage technique that was also being used in the new art of moving pictures comes *The Waste Land* and *The Cantos* and most of the modernist monuments. But Emily Dickinson understood very well how parataxis works from reading the Bible, where it is used to the same purposes she uses it: for the power of compression and giving the narrative progression a feeling of authority and inevitability, especially the narratives of otherworldly travels in her favorite prophetic books, Isaiah and Revelation, that may have sparked the idea for "I heard a fly buzz - when I died" and some of her many other wild stories. Speech is also paratactic, whereas discursive prose tends to be hypotactic: through parataxis we feel the pulse of the speaker, the power of one person talking to another. This is the power she experienced in the many sermons she listened to—Puritan sermons in the tradition of Jonathan Edwards, not Unitarian sermons of rational argument in Higginson's Cambridge. The sermons Emily Dickinson heard were meant to make the listener see and feel the presence of God through the power of God's word, and they used the Biblical rhetoric of parallelism, paradox, and aphorism Dickinson made use of in her poems. And, whereas the sermon was the climax of the religious service, the service was punctuated throughout by hymns, often by Isaac Watts, which Dickinson adapted for her poems with remarkable flexibility, ingenuity, and variety. Against the disjunctions of her grammar between and within sentences, and despite the difficulty of what she is saying, there is always a solidity of form, reinforced and played against, that grounds us in rhythm and sound. She was a master technician. The fundamental regularity of the meter, integrity of the stanza, and correspondence of phrase units with lines that rhyme from slight to full, allow her, through the agency of the famous dashes she borrowed from Watts's hymns, "ungrammatical" movements within and between sentences that unhinge the way words can be used and the world can be seen. As Louise Bogan said, her poems "define and express the very nearly indefinable and inexpressible."

This was a Poet -
It is That
Distills amazing sense
From Ordinary Meanings -
And Attar so immense

From the familiar species
That perished by the Door -
We wonder it was not Ourselves
Arrested it - before -

Of Pictures, the Discloser -
The Poet - it is He -
Entitles Us - by Contrast -
To ceaseless Poverty -

Of Portion - so unconscious -
The Robbing - could not harm -
Himself - to Him - a Fortune -
Exterior - to Time -

446 [#448] (1862)

Dickinson's poetic technique, like that of all the best poets, is an embodied expression of belief. Walt Whitman fashioned what he called a "clear plate-glassy style" for *Leaves of Grass* because he wanted his poem to present "ultimate vivification to facts" that would "make every man his own priest" and "give good heart," thus uniting all people of "these United States" and everyone for all time. Now there was a man with ambition. In 1862, the same year Dickinson first wrote to Higginson, she wrote "my business is Circumference," and, within months, to another correspondent, "my business is to love . . . my business is to sing." She was certainly thinking about her businesses, and of course they are not three businesses but one. She wanted to see as much as she could, love as much as she could, and sing as much as she could. This was her vocation, which was everything, not her career, which was zip. She reminds us in no uncertain terms of the distinction between them and how valuable for a writer keeping that distinction clear can be, especially in our age of celebrity worship when we hear hundreds of thousands of commercials by the time we're twenty-one instead of fifteen hundred sermons. Her poetry was a form of love, her poems instruments for enlightenment and occasions of prayer. For her the poetic enterprise was as private as Whitman's was public, and she found the style that would suit her purpose. It is an inimitable style in a way that Whitman's obviously is not, having been used with varying degrees of success over the years by poets as different as Vachel Lindsay, Kenneth Fearing, Allen Ginsberg, and Gerald Stern. Emily Dickinson is unique because of the degree to which she was able to use what *she* knew, including what she knew with remarkable clarity about herself, to make her poems breathe. The lesson she teaches us is not how to do it but how she did it, not how to do it the way she did it but that it must be done. Against all the blinding power of contemporary conventions very different from those of Emily Dickinson's Amherst but nonetheless every bit as blinding, to see clear to the truth beyond oneself is still the poet's job and very great privilege.

I dwell in Possibility -
A fairer House than Prose -
More numerous of Windows -
Superior - for Doors -

Of Chambers as the Cedars -
Impregnable of Eye -
And for an Everlasting Roof
The Gambrels of the Sky -

Of Visitors - the fairest -
For Occupation - This -
The spreading wide my narrow Hands
To gather Paradise -

                    466 [#657] (1862)

ACKNOWLEDGMENTS

Many of the essays in this book began as lectures to the MFA Program for Writers at Warren Wilson College. The privilege of being part of a community dedicated to excellent writing I owe to Ellen Bryant Voigt, who founded it and whose spirit sustains it. Her response to these essays was characteristically rigorous and generous. I'm also grateful to Jim McMichael, my colleague in the MFA Program at the University of California at Irvine, for translating the idea that my writing is part of my job into time to do it, and for helping me work out in conversation the largest ideas that undergird this work. Stephen Berg published many of these essays in *American Poetry Review* or commissioned them for anthologies, and also helped me over the years to examine assumptions and articulate principles. To these three great friends, for their faith, support, and many many hours of conversation about poetry, this book is dedicated.

My thanks, too, to other beloved friends who read this manuscript in earlier versions and offered suggestions I used: Charles Baxter, Reginald Gibbons, Louise Glück, Robert Pinsky, Melanie Thernstrom, and Geoffrey Wolff.

I'm grateful to the English Department and the MFA Program at the University of California at Irvine for both sanction and sanctuary, and to the gifted graduate students at Irvine who have brought all of themselves to seminars and workshops and contributed to an atmosphere of collaboration instead of competition in which I continue to learn.

Thanks is also due to the Guggenheim Foundation, the Whiting Foundation, and the NEA for their support during this book's initial stages, to the Borchard Foundation for a Fellowship I used in part to reread Emily Dickinson's work, and to the UC Regents for Faculty Research Grants to finish this book. Thanks also to Ruth Anderson Barnett for her help in preparing the manuscript for publication.

To my editor, Barbara Ras, and my agent, Chuck Verrill: thanks for encouraging my vocation and forgiving my career.

And to my wife, Doreen Gildroy, for your love, wisdom, and strength: thank you, dear, now and forever.

Thanks also to all the editors of the following magazines and anthologies where these essays first appeared (sometimes in earlier versions under different titles): *American Poetry Review; Certain Solitudes: On the Poetry and Prose of Donald Justice* (Dana Gioia and William Logan, eds., University of Arkansas Press, 1997); *Claims for Poetry* (Donald Hall, ed., University of Michigan Press, 1982); *Graywolf Forum Three: The Art of Remembering in an Age of Forgetting* (Charles Baxter, ed., Graywolf Press, 1999); *Influence and Mastery* (Stephen Berg, ed., Paul Dry Books, 1999); *New England Review/Bread Loaf Quarterly; Poetics: Essays on the Art of Poetry* (Paul Mariani and George Murphy, eds., Wampeter Press, 1984); *Poetry; Poetry East; Poets Teaching Poets* (Gregory Orr and Ellen Bryant Voigt, eds., University of Michigan Press, 1996); *Singular Voices* (Stephen Berg, ed., Avon, 1985); *The Threepenny Review; TriQuarterly* and *The Writer's Chronicle*.

INDEX

The Life of Poetry
POETS ON THEIR ART AND CRAFT

Carl Dennis
Poetry as Persuasion

Michael Ryan
A Difficult Grace: On Poets, Poetry, and Writing

Sherod Santos
A Poetry of Two Minds

Ellen Bryant Voigt
The Flexible Lyric

MICHAEL RYAN is a professor of English and creative writing at the University of California at Irvine. He earned his M.F.A. and Ph.D. at the University of Iowa and has also taught writing and literature at Princeton University, the University of Virginia, and the MFA Program for Writers at Warren Wilson College. Among the many distinctions for his poetry are the Lenore Marshall Prize, a National Book Award nomination, a Whiting Writers Award, NEA and Guggenheim Fellowships, and the Yale Series of Younger Poets Award, as well as awards from the Poetry Society of America, *American Poetry Review, Ploughshares,* and *Virginia Quarterly Review.* His autobiography, *Secret Life,* was a New York Times Notable Book for 1995. *A Difficult Grace* is the result of studies of poetry, poets, and writing which have appeared widely in magazines and anthologies over the last twenty years.